Praise
*Luther's Smal*
*A Manual for Discipleship*

For Pless, the Small Catechism is no dreary, lifeless, ancient artifact to be memorized at fourteen and then forgotten for the rest of your life. Instead, it holds the answer to renewal in the church today. The remedy for the church's current enervation is not to be found in sleek, high-resolution programs but instead in embracing the Gospel found in the Catechism as a guide for Christ-centered living. Eschewing both the legalism of the evangelical right and the libertinism of the mainline left, Pless portrays Luther's view of discipleship as resilient in the face of spiritual trial, drawn from Christ's very own holiness, which claims every inch of a sinner. Not to be pitted against grace, discipleship directs Christians to serve others even as Christ has served them.

**DR. MARK MATTES,**
PROFESSOR OF THEOLOGY AND PHILOSOPHY,
GRAND VIEW UNIVERSITY

Pless draws on his own experience living out and living out of Luther's Small Catechism; on his years of instructing children, converts, and seminarians; and on the insights of a number of other scholars to help readers put Luther's Catechism to daily use as an excellent field manual for finding Christ's path of discipleship through the shifting sands and dense jungles of modern life. His questions for further reflection and study present a well-designed theologically and pastorally sensitive catechetical course in themselves, which will lead those who put this field manual to work in their lives into a deeper knowledge of Scripture and love of their Lord.

**ROBERT KOLB,**
PROFESSOR OF SYSTEMATIC THEOLOGY EMERITUS,
CONCORDIA SEMINARY, ST. LOUIS

Pless's *A Manual for Discipleship* sheds light on the narrow, sometimes shadowy path between two types of glitzy triumphalism. It's the path of following Christ so closely that we suffer the very attacks that are directed at Him. But the author shows how, with the divine gifts described in Luther's Small Catechism, the Christian can withstand those attacks and persist to the end. What a wonderful guide in the true life of a disciple of Christ.

REV. DR. JACOB CORZINE,
ASSISTANT PROFESSOR OF THEOLOGY,
CONCORDIA UNIVERSITY CHICAGO

With *Luther's Small Catechism: A Manual for Discipleship*, John Pless once again blesses the church, her pastors, and her parents with a uniquely profound examination of the Catechism, unearthing its treasures by setting forth its eternal truths as a field manual for disciples. As he exemplifies in his teaching and living, so does Pless elucidate in his writing how the life of discipleship is one of continual catechesis, never growing out of but rather growing into a life that is given and guided by the Catechism.

REV. PETER J. BROCK,
ST. JOHN LUTHERAN CHURCH, DECATUR, IN

In this book, John T. Pless does us a great service, unpacking the Catechism and its implications for the Christian life. Laypeople and pastors alike will find this to be a very helpful and edifying resource—rooted in the Gospel, clear, biblical, and deserving of several readings and sharing with neighbors.

DR. WADE JOHNSTON,
ASSISTANT PROFESSOR OF THEOLOGY,
WISCONSIN LUTHERAN COLLEGE

# Luther's Small Catechism

## A Manual for Discipleship

## John T. Pless

CONCORDIA PUBLISHING HOUSE · SAINT LOUIS

## Concordia
### Publishing House

Founded in 1869 as the publishing arm of The Lutheran
Church—Missouri Synod, Concordia Publishing House gives
all glory to God for the blessing of 150 years of opportunities
to provide resources that are faithful to the Holy Scriptures
and the Lutheran Confessions.

Published by Concordia Publishing House
3558 S. Jefferson Ave., St. Louis, MO 63118–3968
1-800-325-3040 • cph.org

1  2  3  4  5  6  7  8  9  10          28  27  26  25  24  23  22  21  20  19

# Contents

PREFACE . . . . . . . . . . . . . . . . . . . . . . . . . . . . . . . . . . . . . . . . . . . . . . . ix

**CHAPTER 1**

What Does the Catechism Have to Do with Discipleship? . . . . . . . . .1

**CHAPTER 2**

The Ten Commandments: Path of Discipleship . . . . . . . . . . . . . . .21

**CHAPTER 3**

The Creed: Disciples Confess the Faith . . . . . . . . . . . . . . . . . . . . . .49

**CHAPTER 4**

The LORD's Prayer: Jesus Teaches His Disciples to Pray . . . . . . . . . . .75

**CHAPTER 5**

Holy Baptism: How Disciples Are Made and Kept . . . . . . . . . . . . .101

**CHAPTER 6**

Confession and Absolution:
Disciples Live by the Forgiveness of Sins . . . . . . . . . . . . . . . . . . . .117

**CHAPTER 7**

The Sacrament of the Altar:
Disciples Are Strengthened by Christ's Body and Blood . . . . . . . .129

**CHAPTER 8**

Daily Prayers: Disciples Thank and Praise the Holy Trinity . . . . . .147

**CHAPTER 9**

Table of Duties: Disciples in the World . . . . . . . . . . . . . . . . . . . . . .159

**APPENDIX**

Catechesis for Life in the Royal Priesthood . . . . . . . . . . . . . . . . . .171

**BIBLIOGRAPHY FOR FURTHER STUDY OF THE CATECHISM** . . . . . . . . .196

# Preface

**Where you see and hear the Lord's Prayer prayed and taught; or psalms or other spiritual songs sung, in accordance with the word of God and the true faith; also the creed, the Ten Commandments, and the catechism used in public, you may rest assured that a holy Christian people of God are present.**

Martin Luther, *On the Councils and the Church*
(AE 41:164)

Discipleship is not an extraterrestrial activity. To be a disciple of Jesus Christ is not to escape the world and all that is involved with life on this earth. Looking forward to that city, whose builder and maker is God, as even now we live by faith in the One who has gone before us, we walk with feet firmly planted here in time and space. Martin Luther recognized that the God who created the heavens and the earth is no distant deity but is, literally, a down-to-earth God who formed Adam from the dust of the earth and took on flesh and blood in the womb of Mary to be our Brother and Redeemer.

The crown jewel of the multitude of Luther's writings is without a doubt the Small Catechism, where the Reformer provides disciples with a basic handbook of Christian faith and life. The Formula of Concord called it "the Bible of the laity." Ludwig Ihmels dubbed it a "life book" Other accolades would accrue for this compact book so rich in doctrine and at the same time focused on fundamental questions of life and death.

In an earlier book, *Praying Luther's Small Catechism*, I sought to examine the Catechism through the lens of prayer while making some suggestions as to how its parts might be transfigured into prayer. In this current book, I am suggesting that we might see the Catechism as a field manual for disciples. The image of a field manual is appropriate for soldiers and others whose work takes them into unknown terrain. A field manual imparts essential wisdom for those who would live and work away from the confines of the familiar. It provides directions to ensure survival. It orients those who use it to the conditions specific to the particular environment. A field manual is also appropriate for disciples who live in a world created by God, who have fallen into sin but are reconciled to the Father by the blood of His Son and even now are awaiting the consummation of all things in His return. It orients us to the territory of creation, guarding us from confusing the creature with the Creator.

Christians are, according to Luther, "eternal pupils." That is, we are disciples. Disciples are learners. Our curriculum is straightforward. We need to learn how to receive (faith) and how to give (love). As we live in the field, the Catechism tutors us in both receiving and giving, in both faith and love. All that we have—body and soul—comes from the hand of a generous Creator. The Creator became a creature of our flesh and blood to redeem us from sin, death, and the devil. The good news of this redemption was brought to us in the words of the Spirit.

> **Christians are, according to Luther, "eternal pupils."**

The Spirit enables us to call God "our Father" with the boldness and certainty born of faith. Baptized in the name of the Father, Son, and Holy Spirit, we have died with Christ and so live with Him as we await the resurrection of our bodies. In the meantime, we live in repentance and faith, confessing our sin and receiving the absolution from Christ Himself on the lips of His servant. In the Sacrament of the Altar, Christ Jesus comes to us with His body and blood for the forgiveness of our sin, strengthening us in the life and salvation He acquired for us on Calvary. Strengthened by His testament, we now "thank and praise, serve and obey" our Father, coming to Him in daily prayer and living according to His Commandments in our earthly callings within the congregation, civic community, and household. This is the life of discipleship.

In the nineteenth century, Kahnis observed that "the Small Catechism became the people's book in a manner not achieved by any other book except the Bible."[1] We continue to teach it in our congregations, homes, and schools with the prayer that ordinary Christians will continue to grow up and into the Catechism. What Helmut Thielicke says of young theological students may also be applied to ordinary Christians:

> There is a hiatus between the arena of the young theologian's actual spiritual growth and what he already knows intellectually about this arena. So to speak, he has been fitted like a country boy, with breeches that are too big, into which he must still grow up in the same way that one who is to be confirmed must also still grow into the long trousers of the Catechism. Meanwhile, they hang loosely around his body, and this ludicrous sight is of course not beautiful.[2]

The Catechism is both simple and complex. It takes a lifetime to "fill it out" as disciples continue to mature.

It is my hope that this book will assist ordinary Christians to live as continual disciples, growing in the knowledge of His saving Word. Luther did not see his Catechism as an end in itself but as a handbook that would accompany the Christian, navigating a path through this world with eyes fixed on Jesus, the pioneer and perfecter of our faith. All disciples are in fact theologians, handling

---

1   Cited by W. T. Dau, "How Can We Prove Our Gratitude for Luther's Small Catechism," *Lutheran School Journal* (Summer 1929): 10.

2   Helmut Thielicke, *A Little Exercise for Young Theologians,* trans. Charles L. Taylor (Grand Rapids: Eerdmans, 1962), 28–29.

God's Word as they hear it, receive it in faith, meditate on it, pray from it, and live under the cross that it inevitably brings. To that end, *Luther's Small Catechism: A Manual for Discipleship* is offered as a "catechetical systematics" fleshing out of Luther's teaching of God's Word for twenty-first-century Christians.

While working on this book, I was also serving on the committee to revise *Luther's Small Catechism with Explanation* (CPH, 2017). At the end of each chapter, I have included study and discussion questions for you to make connections with particular aspects of the newly revised Catechism in the hope that this book might serve as something of a companion piece for those who use this edition of the Catechism in their home, congregation, and classroom, as well as for devotional reading.

I dedicate this book to the students who have studied the Catechism with me at Concordia Theological Seminary, Fort Wayne, Indiana, and Lutheran Theological Seminary in Pretoria, South Africa. Their insights and questions have led me deeper into the truth confessed in the Catechism and its utility not only in teaching but also for preaching and pastoral care.

My thanks to Dr. Mark C. Mattes of Grandview University in Des Moines whose insights into the Lutheran character of discipleship were an impulse for the writing of this book.

John T. Pless
April 24, 2019, Wednesday in the Week of
the Resurrection of our Lord

# Chapter 1

⊱⊰

# What Does the Catechism Have
# to Do with Discipleship?

The most effective tool in establishing and structuring the evangelical church in the long term was Luther's Small Catechism (*Der kleine Katechismus*), in effect a manual for Christian faith and life.

HEINZ SCHILLING[3]

*D*iscipleship is a good New Testament word that has enjoyed a resurgence of usage in recent years. It has become part of the name of one denomination, Disciples of Christ, and in some church-growth literature it has become fashionable to distinguish between members and disciples. In a recent article on "Discipleship in Lutheran Perspective,"[4] Mark Mattes suggests that in American Christianity discipleship is broadly understood in two ways. On the one hand, there is the approach of American Evangelicalism, where the tactics of neo-revivalism are employed to provide nominal church members with disciplines that will lead to an experience of God and make for a more effective personal spiritual life. On the other side of the aisle are the mainline churches associated with the Social Gospel movement, where discipleship is

---

3   Heinz Schilling, *Martin Luther: Rebel in an Age of Upheaval*, trans. Rona Johnston (Oxford: Oxford University Press, 2017), 375.

4   See Mark C. Mattes, "Discipleship in Lutheran Perspective," in *The Mercy of God in the Cross of Christ: Essays on Mercy in Honor of Glenn Merritt*, ed. Ross E. Johnson and John T. Pless (St. Louis: The Lutheran Church—Missouri Synod, 2016), 501–18.

defined as moral deliberation that leads to the embrace of a liberal agenda for global justice, peace, and ecological awareness. The approach of American Evangelicalism would fix the church, while the Social Gospel approach would fix the world. Mattes asserts that Lutherans have a completely different take on discipleship, and it has to do with repentance and faith, death and resurrection. Discipleship is about death to the old Adam and the resurrection of a new man, who lives before God by faith and before the world in love that serves the neighbor.

Discipleship is catechetical. It is coherent with the shape and content of Martin Luther's Small Catechism. Friedrich Mildenberger aptly notes, "A catechism is not primarily a book. . . . Rather, catechism is training in a certain body of knowledge."[5] Prior to the Reformation, the term "catechism" was used in a variety of ways inclusive of the core Christian texts of the Creed, Lord's Prayer, and Commandments and the ways in which these texts were taught. We can observe this usage also in Luther. For example, in his Preface to *The German Mass* (1526), Luther writes, "The German service needs a plain and simple, fair and square catechism. Catechism means the instruction in which the heathen who want to be Christians are taught and guided in what they should believe, know, do, and leave undone, according to the Christian faith. This is why the candidates who had been admitted for such instruction and learned the Creed before their Baptism used to be called *catechumenos*. This instruction or catechization I cannot put better or more plainly than has been done from the beginning of Christendom and retained till now, i.e. , in these three parts: the Ten Commandments, the Creed, and the Our Father. These three plainly and briefly contain exactly everything that a Christian needs to know" (AE 53:64–65). Then Luther goes on to suggest how these texts should be taught in the homes in order to train as Christians the children and servants (AE 53:65).

---

5    Friedrich Mildenberger, *Theology of the Lutheran Confessions,* trans. Erwin Lueker (Philadelphia: Fortress Press, 1986), 140.

In his lectures the next year (1527) on the Book of Zechariah, Luther complains that so few preachers properly understand the Lord's Prayer, Creed, and Commandments and are able to teach them to the ordinary folk. Then he goes on to say, "One ought, however, to regard those teachers as the best and the paragons of their profession who present the catechism well—that is, who teach properly the Our Father, the Ten Commandments, and the Creed. But such teachers are rare birds. For there is neither great glory nor outward show in their kind of teaching; but there is in it great good and also the best of sermons, because in this teaching, there is comprehended, in brief, all Scripture. There is no Gospel, either, from which a man could not teach these things if he only were willing and took an interest in teaching the poor common man. One must, of course, constantly prompt the people in these brief things—that is, in the Our Father, the Ten Commandments, and the Creed—and then insist on them and urge them upon the people in all Gospels and sermons" (AE 20:157).

> **In this teaching, there is comprehended, in brief, all Scripture.**

Catechisms sermons were a regular feature of church life in Wittenberg in the 1520s. These sermons reflect the aim of the first of Luther's "Invocavit Sermons," preached after Luther returned from the Wartburg to do damage control on Karlstadt's ill-fated attempt to accelerate reform. In a stunning sentence, Luther sets the reality of death before the congregants: "The summons of death comes to us all, and no one can die for another. Every one must fight his own battle with death by himself, alone. We can shout into another's ears, but every one must himself be prepared for the time of death, for I will not be with you then, nor you with me" (AE 51:70). Then Luther makes the point as to the necessity of catechetical instruction if disciples are to face death in faith: "Therefore everyone must himself know and be armed with the chief things which concern a Christian" (AE 51:70). These chief things that concern a Christian are the stuff of the Catechism. While not Catechism sermons in the narrow sense of that genre, the Invocavit sermons are surely catechetical in that they teach Christians how to live in faith and love, exercising patience in suffering and being well-versed in the Scriptures in order to endure the devil's attacks.

Luther's third series of sermons on the Catechism preached from November 30 to December 18, 1528, prefigures the content of the Large Catechism, even as it demonstrates the seriousness with which Luther took the tasks of teaching disciples of Jesus Christ. In the first of these sermons, Luther reminds his hearers that those who want to be Christian should know the catechism: "And one who does not know them should not be counted among the number of Christians" (AE 51:137). Those who do not know the Catechism are not to be admitted to Holy Communion. In this sermon, Luther also accents the responsibility of parents in partnering with pastors to catechize the young. "Every father of a family is a bishop in his house and the wife a bishopess. Therefore remember that you in your homes are to help us carry on the ministry as we do in the church" (AE 51:137). Luther suggests that the words of the Ten Commandments, the Creed, and the Lord's Prayer can be learned "easily enough by praying in the morning when you rise, in the evening when you go to bed, and before and after meals" (AE 51:137). Learned by heart, these core texts can then be fleshed out with additional biblical passages and the content made explicit in preaching as we see Luther doing in the Catechism sermons.

The recognition of the need for a Catechism and competent catechists, that is, preachers who could prepare the head of the family to teach the faith to his household, became even more urgent with the Saxon Visitation. Along with other Wittenberg colleagues, Luther participated as a "visitor" in the Saxon Visitation of 1528. By his own admission, the bleak conditions in church life compelled him to prepare what we now know as the Small Catechism:

> The deplorable, wretched deprivation that I recently encountered while I was a visitor has constrained and compelled me to prepare this catechism, or Christian instruction, in such a brief, plain, and simple version. Dear God, what misery I beheld! The ordinary person, especially in the villages, knows absolutely nothing about the Christian faith, and unfortunately many pastors are completely unskilled and incompetent teachers. Yet supposedly they all bear the name Christian, are baptized, and receive the holy sacrament, even though they do not know the Lord's Prayer, the Creed, or the Ten Commandments! As a result they live like simple cattle or irrational pigs, and despite the fact that the gospel has returned, have mastered the fine art of misusing all their freedom.
>
> (SC Preface 1–3; K-W, 347–48)

Luther recognized that both pastors and people needed a form of basic instruction in discipleship, for disciples are those who continue in Christ's Word (see John 8:31) and so live not in fleshly bondage to any idolatry but in the freedom He gives.

Luther holds pastors accountable for teaching. In the Preface to the Small Catechism, he challenges pastors and preachers, begging them for God's sake to take up their office, have mercy on their people, and "help us bring the catechism to the people, especially to the young" (SC Preface 6; K-W, 348). Preachers are themselves not only to teach the Catechism but to also grow in their knowledge of it. Like all disciples, pastors are to be "eternal students" who grow ever deeper in the words that they are called to proclaim. In his 1530 Preface to the Large Catechism, Luther confesses,

> But this I say for myself: I am also a doctor and a preacher, just as learned and experienced as all of them who are so high and mighty. Nevertheless, each morning, and whenever else I have time, I do as a child who is being taught the catechism and I read and recite word for word the Lord's Prayer, the Ten Commandments, the Creed, the Psalms, etc. I must still read and study the catechism daily, and yet I cannot master it as I wish, but must remain a child and pupil of the catechism—and I also do so gladly. These fussy, fastidious fellows would like quickly, with one reading, to be doctors above all doctors, to know it all and to need nothing more. Well this, too, is a sure sign that they despise both their office and their people's souls, yes, even God and his Word. They do not need to fall, for they have already fallen all too horribly. What they need, however, is to become children and again begin to learn the ABCs, which they think they have long since outgrown.
>
> (LC PREFACE 7–8; K-W, 380–81)[6]

Recognizing that the Spirit works only through the external words of God to make and sustain disciples of Jesus Christ, Luther is incessant in his insistence that pastors use the Catechism to teach the faith.

Perhaps Luther is so strong in this insistence because he recognizes how multidimensional the Catechism actually is, and this increases its *usefulness* for the life of discipleship. The Small Catechism is multifaceted. Eric Gritsch has called it a "whetstone"[7]

---

6    Also note Albrecht Peters: "The Reformation has placed the catechism again on the lamp stand. . . . After all, all the writings of the Church fathers do not afford such clarity as could be concentrated in the Small Catechism. This is why the reformer, together with those charges learning their ABC's, patiently and continually wants to suckle these central words of God and remain daily 'the catechism's student,'" in *Commentary on Luther's Catechisms: Ten Commandments,* trans. Holger K. Sonntag (St. Louis: Concordia Publishing House, 2009), 35.

7    Eric Gritsch, "Luther's Catechisms of 1529: Whetstones of the Church," *Lutheran Theological Seminary Bulletin* 60 (1980): 3–14.

for the Church as it sharpens basic distinctions necessary for Christian proclamation and life. Kirsi Stjerna identifies it as a "compass,"[8] for it navigates the Christian's reading of Scripture. Charles Arand says that the Small Catechism is a "theological Swiss Army knife,"[9] for it can be used for several tasks. The Small Catechism is a handbook in doctrine, summarizing the Scriptures' teaching of human sin and God's mercy in Christ. It serves as a prayer book. Ludwig Ihmels opined that "the Catechism is not only a school book, and not only a confessional book but it is a life book."[10]

The Catechism (i.e., the Decalogue, Apostles' Creed, Lord's Prayer, and Words of Institution for Baptism and the Lord's Supper) is seen by Luther as a digest and summary of the entire Bible. Already in the "Booklet for the Laity and Children" prepared in Wittenberg in 1525, the Ten Commandments, Creed, Lord's Prayer, and Words of Institution for Baptism and the Sacrament of the Altar are identified as the "Lay Bible."[11] Later on, in 1577, the Epitome of the Formula of Concord calls Luther's Small and Large Catechisms "a Bible of the Laity, in which everything is summarized that is treated in detail in Holy Scripture and that is necessary for a Christian to know for salvation" (FC Ep 5; K-W, 487).

Luther did not see the Small Catechism as a replacement for the Holy Scriptures but as the means to get to their heart and center, Jesus Christ, God's Son in human flesh crucified for the sins of the world and raised from the dead for our justification. The Small Catechism navigates readers of the Bible, guiding them in a reading that is able to distinguish God's threats from His

---

8   Kirsi I. Stjerna, "The Large Catechism of Dr. Martin Luther, 1529," in *Word and Faith*, vol. 2 of *The Annotated Luther*, ed. Kirsi I. Stjerna (Minneapolis: Fortress Press, 2015), 285.

9   Charles Arand, *That I May Be His Own: An Overview of Luther's Catechisms* (St. Louis: Concordia Publishing House, 2000), 57.

10   Cited by J. Michel Reu, *Dr. Martin Luther's Small Catechism: A History of Its Origin, Its Distribution, and Its Use* (Chicago: Wartburg Press, 1929), 366.

11   For the text of "A Booklet for Laity and Children," see *Sources and Context of The Book of Concord*, ed. Robert Kolb and James Nestingen (Minneapolis: Fortress Press, 2001), 1–12.

promises so that faith is anchored in Christ alone. As Mary Jane Haemig puts it, "Learning the catechism was never an end in itself but rather a beginning of a more broad and profound exploration of the Bible and the Christian faith."[12] We can observe this pattern in Luther's Preface to the Small Catechism as he directs users to learn the words, move from the words to the meaning, and then take up a larger Catechism.

In his Preface to the Large Catechism, Luther speaks of a single part of the Catechism, the Ten Commandments, as a "brief digest and summary of the entire Holy Scriptures" (LC Preface 18; K-W, 382). The Reformer says that "those who know the Ten Commandments perfectly know the entire Scriptures and in all affairs and circumstances are able to counsel, help, comfort, judge, and make decisions in both spiritual and temporal matters" (LC Preface 17; K-W, 382). This is not a reduction of Holy Scripture but a way of reading the Bible from these core texts. Already in his *Personal Prayer Book* of 1522, Luther anticipated the ordering of the first three parts of the Small Catechism:

> **"Those who know the Ten Commandments perfectly know the entire Scriptures.**

> Three things a person must know in order to be saved. First, he must know what to do and what to leave undone. Second, when he realizes that he cannot measure up to what he should do or leave undone, he needs to know where to go to find the strength he requires. Third, he must know how to seek and obtain that strength. It is just like a sick person who first has to determine the nature of his sickness, then find out what to do or to leave undone. After that he has to know where to get the medicine which will help him do or leave undone what is right for a healthy person.

---

12    Mary Jane Haemig, "An Image of Luther for Today: The Catechetical Luther," *Word & World* 36 (Spring 2016): 124.

**Then he has to desire to search for this medicine and to obtain it or have it brought to him.**

(AE 43:13)

This would lead Luther to shift the structure of the sequence of the three core texts in catechetical instruction. Until the middle of the fifteenth century, the sequence of Creed-Our Father-Decalogue dominates. Around 1450, the Our Father takes the first position in catechetical handbooks. Johannes Surgant (1450–1503) gives rationale for the medieval sequence of Our Father-Creed-Ten Commandments in his *Manuale curatorum:*

> **Since prayer that is not prayed in true faith is without power (for without faith no one pleases God), recite the Creed. Since faith without works is totally without any power and dead and comes to be alive only through obedience to the Ten Commandments, therefore obey the Ten Commandments and learn them.**[13]

The popular catechism by Dietrich Kolde (ca. 1435–1515), *A Fruitful Mirror, or Small Handbook for Christians,* organized the parts of the catechism with penance in view. In *A Fruitful Mirror,* the Creed comes first as all Christians could confess it. The Creed was followed by the Commandments and other catalogs of sin as a preparation for confession to the priest. Finally, there is the Lord's Prayer as the prayer to be prayed in order to attain grace.[14]

Luther begins with the Ten Commandments as the summary of God's Law, which structures human life and shows sin. The Commandments are followed by the Creed as an exposition of the trinitarian Gospel. Then comes the Lord's Prayer as the cry of faith in the midst of affliction, imploring God on the basis of

---

13  Gottfried Krodel, "Luther's Work on the Catechism in the Context of Late Medieval Catechetical Literature," *Concordia Journal* 25 (October 1999): 370.

14  Timothy J. Wengert, "The Small Catechism, 1529," in *Pastoral Writings,* vol. 4 of *The Annotated Luther,* ed. Mary Jane Haemig (Minneapolis: Fortress Press, 2016), 202.

His command and promise to deliver and save. James Nestingen observes:

> Luther follows an experiential order. He begins with the commandments because this is where life begins, under the *nomos,* in the context of the demands and conditions that bear down from birth to death. As Luther understands and interprets them, the Ten Commandments codify and summarize the essential requirements of life in relation to both God and the neighbor. The gospel declares that Christ has broken into the world of the law to take it upon himself in his death and resurrection to make sinners his own, thereby freeing them from the powers of sin, death, and the devil. The Lord's Prayer follows the Creed, exposing the shape of life as it is lived out in the tension between the claims of the law and the gospel, teaching sinners to call out to Christ Jesus for his assistance. In this way each of the three parts of the catechism posts a defining part of the life of faith—demand, gift, and consolation in the struggles of life.[15]

To this catechetical core, Luther will add material on Baptism and the Lord's Supper and eventually on Confession and Absolution to teach not only what the Sacraments are but how they are to be used as faith lays hold of the treasures God gives in them.

**Disciples are those people who are called to faith by the Gospel and now, living by the promises of Christ, take up the cross and follow Him.**

Disciples are those people who are called to faith by the Gospel and now, living by the promises of Christ, take up the cross and follow Him. Luther does not envision the Christian life—that is, the life

---

15    James A. Nestingen, *The Lutheran Confessions: History and Theology of the Book of Concord* (Minneapolis: Fortress Press, 2012), 76.

of discipleship—without the cross. In his exposition of the Third Petition in the Large Catechism, Luther writes

> For where God's Word is preached, accepted, or believed, and bears fruit, there the holy and precious cross will also not be far behind. And let no one think that he will have peace; rather, we must sacrifice all we have on earth—possessions, honor, house and farm, spouse and children, body and life. Now, this grieves our flesh and the old creature, for it means that we must remain steadfast, suffer patiently whatever befalls us, and let go whatever is taken from us.
>
> (LC III 65–66; K-W, 448–49)

Oswald Bayer has contrasted Luther's approach to theology with that of Anselm as it was configured in the medieval tradition. For Anselm, theology was faith seeking understanding. For Luther, it was faith enduring attack.[16] In this light, we see Luther's intention in preparing the Catechisms and urging their use by disciples of Jesus Christ, ordinary Christians.

This can be seen explicitly in Luther's Preface to the Large Catechism. Repeatedly, Luther urges Christians not to take the Catechism for granted or to believe that they have attained a sufficient knowledge of the faith. Not the least of Luther's concerns is that Christians are imperiled by the assaults of the devil, the world, and the sinful flesh and cannot withstand these attacks without God's Word:

> Nothing is so powerfully effective against the devil, the world, the flesh, and all evil thoughts as to occupy one's self with God's Word, to speak about it and meditate upon it, in the way that Psalm 1[:2] calls those blessed

---

16   Oswald Bayer, *Theology the Lutheran Way,* trans. Jeffery Silcock and Mark Mattes (Grand Rapids: Eerdmans, 2007), 210–13.

who "meditate on God's law day and night." Without doubt you will offer up no more powerful incense or savor against the devil than to occupy yourself with God's commandments and words and to speak, sing, or think about them.

(LC PREFACE 10; K-W, 381)

If the fact that the devil, who constantly ambushes Christians with his "daily and incessant attacks" (LC Preface 13; K-W, 382), is not enough to drive Christians to use the Catechism, Luther says that we have God's command:

If this were not enough to admonish us to read the catechism daily, God's command should suffice to compel us. For God solemnly enjoins us in Deuteronomy 6[:7–8] that we should meditate on his precepts while sitting, walking, standing, lying down, and rising, and should keep them as an ever-present emblem and sign before our eyes and on our hands. God certainly does not require and command this so solemnly without reason. He knows our danger and need; he knows the constant and furious attacks and assaults of the devil. Therefore, he wishes to warn, equip, and protect us against them with good "armor" against their "flaming arrows," and with a good antidote against their evil infection and poison. Oh, what mad, senseless fools we are! We must ever live and dwell in the midst of such mighty enemies like the devils, and yet we would despise our weapons and armor, too lazy to examine them or give them a thought!

(LC PREFACE 14–15; K-W, 382)

Preachers are warned not to become so vain as to imagine that they have mastered the Catechism and already know all that they need to know. Luther urges preachers to study and mediate on the Catechism so that they, in turn, are able to teach it to those committed to their care. Thus Luther returns to the neediness of common believers:

> **Let all Christians drill themselves in the catechism daily, and constantly put it into practice, guarding themselves with the greatest care and diligence against the poisonous infection of such security or arrogance. Let them constantly read and teach, learn and meditate and ponder. Let them never stop until they have proved by experience and are certain that they have taught the devil to death and have become more learned than God himself and all his saints.**

(LC Preface 19; K-W, 382–83)

The Catechism is the weaponry for spiritual warfare as disciples need to be trained in the use of the Word of God and prayer in the battle against the pressures of the world, the gravitational pull of fallen human nature, and the crafty tactics of the evil one designed to draw us away from the only true God and place trust instead in ourselves or some created thing.

The life of discipleship is oriented by the First Commandment; it is a life of fearing, loving, and trusting in God above all things. This God who is to be feared, loved, and trusted above all things is none other than the triune God. He is the one God who is Father, Son, and Holy Spirit as confessed in the Creed. He is the God who has created us and all that exists, redeemed us with the suffering and death of His Son, sanctified us by the Spirit's Gospel to live as His own. Each article of the Creed ends with Luther's signature line: "This is most certainly true." This phrase becomes the platform for our calling Jesus' Father "Our Father" with boldness and confidence. In the Small Catechism, Baptism, Absolution, and the Sacrament of the Altar are not merely an

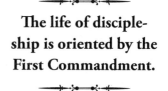

**The life of discipleship is oriented by the First Commandment.**

addendum to the catechetical core of Decalogue, Creed, and Lord's Prayer. They are necessarily connected to the confession of the Third Article, particularly the line that reads "Daily in this Christian church the Holy Spirit abundantly forgives all sins—mine and those of all believers" (SC II 6; K-W, 356). This is made even more explicit in the Large Catechism:

> **Further we believe that in this Christian community we have the forgiveness of sins, which takes place through the holy sacraments and absolution as well as through all the comforting words of the entire gospel. This encompasses everything that is to be preached about the sacraments and, in short, the entire gospel and all the official responsibilities of the Christian community.**
>
> (LC II 54; K-W, 438)

Then a few lines later, Luther writes, "Therefore everything in this Christian community is so ordered that everyone may daily obtain full forgiveness of sins through the Word and signs appointed to comfort and encourage our consciences as long as we live on earth" (LC II 55; K-W, 438). Then to the Small Catechism, Luther adds as appendices daily prayers and the Table of Duties, for it is in daily life that disciples "thank, praise, serve, and obey God." It is within the time and places of life in the world that disciples live. Luther gives expression to this life with Morning and Evening Prayers as well as mealtime prayers. Discipleship is not a withdrawal from this world into a rarified spirituality in a priestly or monastic order; rather, it is life lived in the earthly estates of church, civil community, and household.

Luther recognized that the life of faith in the world is imperiled by false teachers and persecution from those who are enemies of Christ. Training in the Catechism was seen as enabling Christians to distinguish the truth from false and pernicious doctrines that would undermine faith. Teaching the Catechism was also seen as a kind of pre-need pastoral care so that Christians would be ready for trials that might come with persecution. In his 1541 tract *Appeal for Prayer against the Turks*, Luther reminded his readers:

> And finally, I strongly urge that the children be taught the catechism. Should they be taken captive in the invasion, they will at least take something of the Christian faith with them. Who knows what God might be able to accomplish through them. Joseph as a seventeen-year-old youth was sold into slavery into Egypt, but he had God's word and knew what he believed.
>
> (AE 43:239)

Disciples are to be prepared for whatever trials yet await them in the future. If the Catechism is engraved in the memory and embedded in the heart, then disciples will carry with them all they need to remain faithful to their Lord.

J. Michel Reu has documented how Luther's Small Catechism was taught and used from the sixteenth century into the early decades of the twentieth century. One aspect of the Small Catechism's usefulness was in mission work. Disciples are made by baptizing and teaching. The historian of Lutheran missions, Ingemar Öberg, notes, "Luther's Small Catechism soon became a standard book for basic Christian instruction in Europe. Its significance for evangelical Lutheran mission work to the present day cannot be overestimated."[17] Swedish pastor John Campanius (1601–83), while serving colonists in New Sweden, south of Philadelphia, found time to learn the language of the Delaware Indians, and he translated the Small Catechism into that tongue in 1697. Bartholomew Ziegenbalg (1682–1719), the first Lutheran missionary to India, translated the Small Catechism into Tamil in

> **Disciples are to be prepared for whatever trials yet await them.**

---

17    Ingemar Öberg, *Luther and World Mission: A Historical and Systematic Study,* trans. Dean Apel (St. Louis: Concordia Publishing House, 2007), 494.

1707 and used it in his missionary efforts. No wonder then that church historian Mark Noll comments, "Much of the influence of Lutheranism around the world can be traced to the success of this catechism in expressing the profound truths of the faith in a language that all can understand."[18]

The Small Catechism is not merely a relic of the sixteenth century. After nearly five hundred years, it has demonstrated its own resilience and durability in Lutheran churches throughout the world. It embodies the central truths of the Reformation in such a way to touch heart and mind, disciplining the Christian in the ongoing life of repentance, faith, and vocation. This is the life of discipleship.

## AN OVERVIEW OF LUTHER'S SMALL CATECHISM WITH EXPLANATION 2017

Already in the sixteenth century, it was common for pastors and teachers to prepare expanded expositions of the text of Luther's Six Chief Parts. The most recent revision, *Luther's Small Catechism with Explanation* (2017), stands within this tradition. Explanations, of course, are reflective of the particular times when they are written, addressing the biblical truth digested in the Small Catechism to the specific issues and challenges of the day. This most recent revision has also structured the explanation in a four-part template: (1) The Central Thought; (2) A Closer Reading of the Small Catechism; (3) Connections and Applications; (4) Psalm, Hymn, and Prayer. This is a feature unique to the 2017 Explanation.

The Appendix of the 2017 Explanation also includes many items that will be helpful for ordinary disciples to better understand and articulate their faith in daily life. Note that page numbers refer to the hardcover edition of the Catechism.

---

18    Mark Noll, *Confessions and Catechisms of the Reformation* (Vancouver: Regent College Press, 2004), 60.

- **Who Is Jesus? How Creeds and Confessions Help Us to Answer This Question (pp. 351–53).** This is a short summary of the origin and purpose of the ecumenical creeds and the Lutheran Confessions.

- **Reading God's Word (pp. 354–57).** This piece lays out five key points to keep in mind when reading the Bible.

- **What Is Worship? (pp. 358–59).** The basic movement in the Lutheran liturgy is God speaking to us in His Word and our responding in confession, prayer, thanksgiving, and praise. The structure of the Lutheran Divine Service keeps this movement in focus.

- **Simple Prayer (pp. 360–61).** Luther's "A Simple Way to Pray," written in 1535 as instruction for his barber, demonstrates how the Catechism can be prayed.

- **Salvation Outline (p. 362).** This provides biblical texts that define human beings' relationship to God under sin and grace. This might be useful for evangelism.

- **Luther's Preface (pp. 363–67).** Luther speaks of the conditions that prompted him to prepare the Small Catechism and how he intended it to be used in congregations and homes.

- **Explanation of Luther's Seal (p. 368).** Luther's words describe how this simple symbol depicts Christian faith.

- **Books of the Bible (pp. 369–71).** This explains the divisions of the Bible and how to pronounce book names.

- **The Times between the Testaments (pp. 372–76).** A short history of what was happening in the four hundred years between the Old and New Testaments.

- **The Church Year (pp. 377–82).** An explanation of what the Church Year is, how it works, and why it is important.

- **Terms Relating to Worship and God's House (pp. 383–86).** A short glossary of words seen in church and used in worship.

- **Symbols and Their Meanings (pp. 387–93).** Pictures and explanations of symbols commonly used in Christian materials.

- **Catechism Glossary (pp. 394–98).** An explanation of words encountered while reading the Catechism.

- **Scriptural Index (pp. 399–421).** This connects specific Bible verses to the Catechism.

- **Index of Topics (pp. 422–429).** This provides a connection between the Catechism and Scripture for certain topics (e.g., abortion, confession, fortune-telling, Islam, liturgy, the return of Christ, suffering).

All this is packed under one cover with Luther's Small Catechism (which is a brief 23 pages long). This additional material may prove useful in continuing to grow in the grace and knowledge of Christ as it is summarized and outlined in Luther's little booklet, for there is always more to learn.

*FOR FURTHER REFLECTION AND STUDY: CONNECTIONS WITH
LUTHER'S SMALL CATECHISM WITH EXPLANATION 2017*

In light of your reading of this chapter, review the Introduction (pp. 43–51) and then reflect on or discuss these questions.

1. How does the Catechism answer the question "What does it mean to be a Christian?"

2. What is faith?

3. How are we to understand discipleship?

4. What does the Bible teach us about its origin and authority?

5. If we have the Bible, why do we need the Catechism?

6. What are the Six Chief Parts of Christian doctrine? Why did Luther arrange them in the order he did? How did Luther's ordering of the Six Chief Parts reflect the distinction between God's Law and His Gospel?

7. How is Jesus Christ at the heart and center of the Catechism?

8. How does the Catechism prepare us to live a "life under attack"?

9. How does the First Commandment give direction to the life of discipleship?

10. What is the significance of the Catechism for mission work? How might you use the Catechism in your own witness to unbelieving friends or family members?

## Chapter 2

---·:·— —·:·—

# The Ten Commandments: Path of Discipleship

Therefore, however long we live, we shall always have our hands full if we remain pupils of the first commandment and of faith throughout all works and sufferings, and never cease to learn. Nobody knows what a great thing it is to trust God alone except him who begins to trust and tries to do faith's works.

Martin Luther, *Treatise on Good Works*
*(1520)* (AE 44:61)

Discipleship consists of fearing, loving, and trusting the one true God above all things. To be a disciple is to have a lord, and this lord is the triune God who has created us, reconciled us to Himself, and hallowed us in body and soul to live as His possession. To fear Him is to live with the recognition that as our Creator, He has authority over our existence, the power to judge us. It is to recognize that He is the One to whom we are accountable. To love Him is to desire Him above all things, to seek no ultimate comfort in any other created being or thing. To trust in Him is to rely solely on His promises in life and in death; it is look to Him for every good thing. Our trust is not in what can be seen but in the God who has identified Himself as our Lord in "the promise of all promises," namely, Exodus 20:2,

"I am the LORD your God." As Bayer puts it, "Trust in the world without trust in God is an illusion."[19]

Trust is the fundamental synonym for faith in Luther's thinking. One is a disciple of whoever or whatever he or she is ultimately trusting in. As Kolb explains it, this trust is inclusive of one's whole being:

> It expresses itself in the emotions, the feelings of peace, joy, delight, and hope from loving God. For Luther, faith or trust included these human actions of understanding, willing and feeling; yet more deeply and completely for him, trust constituted the entire disposition of the individual, of the entire human personality.[20]

Conversely, "Trust in false gods contaminated and corrupted a person's humanity."[21] Faith or trust in the true God comes only through His creative word of promise, the Gospel.

# THE FIRST COMMANDMENT

In the First Commandment, God Himself is speaking.

> Therefore let everyone take this to heart and thus be careful not to regard this as if a mere human being were speaking. For it brings you either eternal blessing, happiness, and salvation, or eternal wrath, distress, and heartache. What more could you want or desire than God's gracious promise that he wants to be yours with every blessing, to protect you, and to help you in every need? Unfortunately, the world neither believes this nor regards it as God's Word. For the world sees that those who trust in God and not in mammon suffer

---

19    Oswald Bayer, "Trust," *Lutheran Quarterly* 24 (2015): 253.

20    Robert Kolb, *Martin Luther and the Enduring Word of God* (Grand Rapids: Baker, 2016), 65.

21    Kolb, *Enduring Word*, 65.

> grief and want and are opposed and attacked by the
> devil. They have neither money, prestige, nor honor,
> and can hardly stay alive. Conversely, those who serve
> mammon have power, prestige, honor, possessions, and
> all sorts of security in the world's eyes. Therefore, we
> must hold fast to these words, even in the face of this
> apparent contradiction, and be certain that they do
> not lie or deceive but will yet prove true.
>
> (LC I 41–42; K-W, 391)

The path of discipleship is dangerous, for it is a road subject
to ambush by our persistent and ever-resilient enemies of the devil,
the world, and our own corrupted nature.
Because what we see and experience with
our own senses seems more real and trustworthy than God Himself, the life of
discipleship calls for discernment. In the

**The path of disciple-
ship is dangerous.**

words of Friedrich Mildenberger, "We thus learn to distinguish
between the illusory world of idolatry that people create for
themselves and the real world established by God."[22]

It is the very nature of idolatry that it is illusory. Our word
*idol* comes from the Greek word *eidolon*, meaning "phantom" or
"image."[23] With the First Commandment, God confiscates the
totality of the disciple's life; He will not share His disciples with
illusory images that promise pleasure but deliver pain, that offer
heaven but subject their followers to hell.

The apostle Paul captures the illusory nature of false gods
in 1 Corinthians in the context of his discussion of eating food
sacrificed in the pagan cults:

---

22    Friedrich Mildenberger, *Theology of the Lutheran Confessions*, 144. Also note the observation by James Nestingen: "An idol abstracts a characteristic of the living God, selecting one out of many and freezes it in an image. Consequently, the idol doesn't give life but draws its life from the ones who worship it; it can't save, but must be saved," "Graven Images and Christian Freedom," *Lutheran Theological Journal* (May 2015): 34.

23    Here see the discussion of Larry Hurtado, *Destroyer of the Gods: Early Christian Distinctiveness in the Roman World* (Waco, TX: Baylor University Press, 2016), 49ff. Also see Michael Lockwood, *The Unholy Trinity: Martin Luther against the Idols of Me, Myself, and I* (St. Louis: Concordia Publishing House, 2016), 21–40.

> We know that "an idol has no real existence," and that
> "there is no God but one." For although there may be
> so-called gods in heaven or on earth—as indeed there
> are many "gods" and many "lords"—yet for us there is
> one God, the Father, from whom are all things and for
> whom we exist, and one Lord, Jesus Christ, through
> whom are all things and through whom we exist.
>
> (1 CORINTHIANS 8:4–6)

In the words of Helmut Thielicke, "For belief in idols does not have its root in the existence of false gods; it is merely a projection of the wandering heart which has fallen victim to blasphemy."[24] God wars against phantoms who are elusive and deceptive. This is why Luther anchors his exposition of the Ten Commandments in the First Commandment.

That on which the heart relies is, in fact, your God. It is faith that makes both God and the idol, Luther writes in the Large Catechism.[25] For Luther, a right understanding of the First Commandment requires the distinction of God's Law from God's Gospel. The First Commandment forbids, prohibits, and condemns trust in anything or anyone other than the God who has made us. This is Law. But there is also good news in the First Commandment because to have the true God by faith is to have the only Lord you need in life and death. Luther put it like this in his exposition of the Penitential Psalms in 1525:

> *For you are my God* [Psalm 143:10]. That is, I do
> not make for myself an idol out of my wisdom and

---

24  Helmut Thielicke, *Theological Ethics*, vol. 1: *Foundations*, ed. William Lazareth (Philadelphia: Fortress Press, 1966), 306.

25  Satan attacks the First Commandment, inciting trust in something other than the triune God. Edmund Schlink describes this seductive assault: "Thus the devil lures men to devise their own gods and cults and he fans into blasphemy and idolatry the small spark of their knowledge that there is a God. . . . He misleads man not only to a corruption of the Decalogue in his thoughts but also to transgressions in the act of murder, adultery, greed etc. Both sins—blasphemies and vices—are inseparably connected; ungodly deeds are produced by ungodly opinions. The devil seduces men by stupefying them. They imagine that they are wise, whereas they go astray as fools, and they think they are good even while they do evil," *Theology of the Lutheran Confessions*, trans. Paul F. Koehneke and Herbert J. A. Bouman (Philadelphia: Fortress Press, 1961), 195.

righteousness, as my enemies do; instead, I cling to Your grace and receive from You wisdom and righteousness, which are found in You and endure forever.

(AE 14:202)

Disciples are those whose lives are oriented by the fear, love, and trust in God above all things. Thus Luther urges Christians:

Learn the First Commandment well, so that we see that God will tolerate no presumption or trust in anything else; he makes no greater demand on us than a heartfelt trust in him for every good thing, so that we walk straight ahead on the right path, using all of God's

> Disciples are those whose lives are oriented by the fear, love, and trust in God above all things.

gifts exactly as a shoemaker uses a needle, awl, and thread for his work and afterward puts them aside, or as a traveler makes use of an inn, food, and lodging, but only for his physical needs. Let each person do the same in his or her walk of life according to God's order, allowing none of these things to be a lord or an idol.

(LC I 47; K-W, 392)

The First Commandment is foundational and essential for disciples of Jesus Christ, for as Luther says, "Out of this commandment flows all the doctrine of the prophets and the psalms as out of a spring and fountain, likewise all curses, threats, and all promises."[26]

The First Commandment overlaps with the First Article for disciples of Jesus Christ, who now live as those who are not of the world but in the world. Discipleship does not draw believers out of the world but turns them into the world to live within

---

26  A. Peters, *Ten Commandments*, 114.

their vocations in the freedom of faith. Such freedom is not the license to do as you please. That would be slavery, bondage to the cruelest of masters—the self. Instead, the freedom of faith gives us the courage to live a life of love for the well-being of our neighbors in this world. Where creation is received as a gift from the Father, it cannot be made into an idol.

With a conscience freed by faith in Christ Jesus, disciples now live within creation according to God's Commandments. Oswald Bayer[27] has observed that in the classical liberalism of the nineteenth century, the ethics of Jesus was touted as an ethic of radical obedience, while the ethics of Paul developed into one governed by the household codes borrowed from antiquity. That is to say that Jesus demanded His disciples to leave house and family, abandoning every domestic tie that would bind them, and to follow Him as spiritual vagabonds. Paul (and those who came after him), on the other hand, expected Christians to live lives of responsibility in their homes and civil communities governed by codes of behavior such as we see in Colossians, Ephesians, and 1 Peter. Liberal theologians of the nineteenth century saw these two approaches in unresolved conflict with each other.

Bayer argues that Luther's approach to ethics is governed by the First Commandment, but unlike the liberal theologians of the nineteenth century, the Reformer sets this commandment not in opposition to responsibilities in creation but within the context of our worldly callings.[28] It is within the congregation, civic government, family, and workplace that the disciple lives the life of fearing, loving, and trusting God above all things. Discipleship is not an extraction from the network of creation with its obligations to other people; rather, discipleship is the life

---

27    See Bayer's discussion of this theme in "Luther's Ethics as Pastoral Care," in *Freedom in Response: Lutheran Ethics; Sources and Controversies*, trans. Jeff Cayzer (Oxford: Oxford University Press, 2007), 119–37.

28    This is affirmed by Udo Schnelle: "The *Haustafel* (household) that concludes the body of the letter (Col. 3:18–4:1) testifies to the fact that the life of the church is still interwoven with the realities of the earthly life," in *Theology of the New Testament*, trans. M. Eugene Boring (Grand Rapids: Baker Academic, 2009), 551.

of faith and love lived out in the structures that Luther identifies as the three estates.

It is in the three estates—the church, the civil community, and the household—that God's commandments govern human life. In the Small Catechism, Luther sees each of the Ten Commandments as not merely prohibitive, forbidding a particular attitude or action but also as enjoining a positive responsibility. The prohibition of idolatry in the First Commandment prescribes faith, that is, we are to fear, love, and trust in God above all things.

## THE SECOND COMMANDMENT

So also in the Second Commandment we learn that disciples are to refrain from cursing, swearing, the practice of magic (satanic arts), lying, and deception by God's name. Instead, God's name is rightly used when we call upon it every trouble, pray, praise, and give thanks. Baptized into God's triune name, disciples have this divine name on their lips. Luther reminds us that "God's name cannot be abused more flagrantly than when it used to lie and deceive" (LC I 53; K-W, 393). When misused in this way, God's name is made a cover and endorsement of the lie, an occasion to "publicly slander the truth and God's Word and consign it to the devil" (LC I 56; K-W, 393). Conversely, when God's Word is taught in truth and purity and His disciples call upon Him as commanded in Psalm 50:15, "Call upon Me in the day of trouble; I will deliver you, and you shall glorify Me," then His name is used as He intended it to be used, that is, to give us access to Himself.[29]

---

29    A. Weiser notes that Psalm 50:15 "refers back to the fundamental theme 'I am the Lord, your God,'" *The Old Testament Library: Psalms*, trans. H. Hartwell (Philadelphia: Westminster Press, 1962), 397. This connection with the prologue of the First Commandment (Ex. 20:1) links the use of God's name to God Himself. Also note the words of Old Testament scholar Gerhard von Rad that "there was a close and essential relationship between it [the name] and its subject [God]," in *Old Testament Theology*, vol. 1, trans. D. M. G. Stalker (New York: Harper and Row, 1962), 181. In his continued discussion of the divine name, von Rad points out that without God's name it is impossible for human beings to invoke Him, hence there could be no worship of God. Here also see A. Peters, "The Prohibition of Abusing the Holy Name in the Old Testament Decalogue," in *Ten Commandments*, 152–54.

# The Third Commandment

Disciples are those who continue in the Lord's Word. Without God's Word, there can be no holy use of God's name. Luther realizes that in its original form, the Third Commandment was given only to Israel, in that God enjoined them to sanctify a particular day, the seventh day, by ceasing from their labor. This is its outward meaning:

> As far as outward observance is concerned, the commandment was given to the Jews alone. They were to refrain from hard work and to rest, so that both human beings and animals might be refreshed and not be exhausted by constant labor.
>
> (LC I 81; K-W, 397)

In Christ, this commandment, like all ritual practices of the old covenant, such as days and ceremonies, find their fulfillment. They are now obsolete, for Christ has come.

Because disciples are sanctified by the true holy thing, the Word of God, they are not made holy by days or seasons, disciplines or spiritual practices:

> For the Word of God is the true holy object above all holy objects. Indeed, it is the only one we Christians know and have. Even if we had the bones of all the saints or all the holy and consecrated vestments gathered together in one pile, they would not help us in the least, for they are all dead things that cannot make anyone holy. But God's Word is the treasure that makes everything holy. By it all the saints have themselves been made holy. At whatever time God's Word is taught, preached, heard, read, or pondered, there the person, the day, and the work is hallowed, not on account of the external work but on account

of the Word that makes us all saints. Accordingly, I constantly repeat that all our life and work must be based on God's Word if they are to be God-pleasing or holy. Where that happens the commandment is in force and is fulfilled. Conversely, any conduct or work apart from God's Word is unholy in the sight of God, no matter how splendid and brilliant it may appear, or even if it is altogether covered with holy relics, as our the so-called spiritual walks of life, which do not know God's Word but seek holiness in their own works.

(LC I 91–93; K-W, 399)

Luther recognizes that nature teaches us that our bodies need rest; according to our Creator's design, we cease work so that the body can relax and be refreshed. Charles Arand summarizes Luther's move in this way:

> The shift to creation as the context allowed Luther to make the point that the Sabbath was made for man and not man for the Sabbath (Mark 2:27). In other words, the Sabbath commandment was not given in order to require our obedience to humanly devised devotional acts. Instead, the observance of the Sabbath was intended to serve the needs of God's human creatures for rest and refreshment.[30]

When it comes to the life of faith, a spiritual Sabbath is necessary so that we might hear the Word of God, which alone bestows life and peace. Such a day is not limited to the seventh day or in the New Testament to Sunday. Hans Wiersma observes, "Luther did not give particular emphasis to Sunday. Instead, by making the Sabbath commandment about the hearing and learning of God's word, Luther in a sense *expanded* the commandment to

---

30    Charles Arand, "Luther's Radical Reading of the Sabbath Commandment," in *Perspectives on the Sabbath: 4 Views*, ed. Christopher John Donato (Nashville: B & H Publishing Group, 2011), 254.

cover *all* days which the word could be heard."[31] The disciple lives in a perpetual Sabbath because he or she lives in the Gospel of Jesus Christ. With His words of spirit and life dwelling in us, we live in Him and have true rest.

Sunday exists for the sake of the sermon. "He [Luther] clearly regarded the sermon as part of Christ's battle against sin and evil; the pulpit is an eschatological battleground where Christ's truth is attacked by and triumphs over the devil's lie."[32] Not only did Luther restore the sermon to its rightful place in the Divine Service, but he also gave preachers practical advice for the construction and delivery of sermons. For Luther, good sermons brought together teaching and exhortation all the while distinguishing between the Law and the promise. "Luther's rule of faith included the proper distinction of law and gospel as the framework for the activity of the text in making its impact on the hearers."[33] The goal of the sermon for Luther was to foster the life of repentance and faith in Christ. Through the preached Word, disciples keep the true Sabbath as they retreat from their own labors and let God speak to them through the voice of the preacher.

Disciples find their rest in Jesus' righteousness, not in their own activities. This righteousness is bestowed through the preaching of God's Word. The Catechism teaches us that we are not to despise it "but hold it sacred and gladly hear and learn it." Apart from God's Word, there is no faith, and where faith is absent, there is no life with God. The life of discipleship is not characterized by endless activity but by returning week after week to gladly hear the Word of life and find in it peace and rest. It has been said that in our day, people work at their play, worship at their work, and play at their worship. Work and the pursuit of leisure are not in and of themselves bad, but they are poor substitutes for God. If they are worshiped in His place, they will disappoint. The Third

---

31    Hans Wiersma, "On Keeping the Sabbath Holy in Martin Luther's Catechism and Other Writings," *Word & World* 36: 3 (Summer 2016): 240.

32    Kolb, *Enduring Word*, 187; also see Paulson/Croghan, Pless

33    Kolb, *Enduring Word*, 188

Commandment orients the time of the disciple back to the First Commandment as we fear and love God so that we cherish His Word and devote time and space to hearing it.

Luther's focus is on God's Word, as it is weaponry against the incessant attacks of the evil one, who ceaselessly attempts to entice Christians away from Christ and His salvation:

> Even though you know the Word perfectly and have already mastered everything, you are daily under the dominion of the devil, and he does not rest day or night in seeking to take you unawares and to kindle in your heart unbelief and wicked thoughts against these three and all the other commandments. Therefore you must constantly keep God's Word in your heart, on your lips, and in your ears. For where the heart stands idle and the Word is not heard, the devil breaks in and does his damage before we realize it. On the other hand, when we seriously ponder the Word, hear it, and put it to use, such is its power that it never departs without fruit.
>
> (LC I 100–101; K-W, 400)

Baptized into Christ's death and resurrection, the disciple remains under attack and finds shelter only in God's Word and also learns how to use the Spirit's sword defensively against Satan and the lies he preaches to the embattled conscience.

# The Fourth Commandment

The Fourth Commandment takes us into discipleship at its most mundane level, life in the family. Oswald Bayer observes that Luther speaks of the Fourth Commandment as "the first and greatest of those commandments that concern earthly life":

> It is related to the place and activity that most undeniably represents my beginning. Thus the fourth

> commandment is "the first and greatest" command-
> ment because it relates to that point at which I was
> called into life by God through my parents—called
> into purely physical, yet at the same time social life. . . .
> I did not choose my parents, the place or language of
> my birth; I was born. As theological language has it: I
> was created; God created me into life, albeit, through
> my parents.[34]

God has given you your parents; it is for this reason they are to be honored.

The commandment to honor father and mother, along with the Sixth Commandment, stands guard over the fundamental bond of marriage and family. Through parents, God brings into existence new human life, guarding, protecting, and nurturing offspring. According to Luther, the majesty of God resides in the parental office, for through them, the Creator is exercising His authority to call life into being and provide order for that life in this world: "God has given this walk of life, fatherhood and motherhood, a special position of honor, higher than any other walk of life under it. Not only has he commanded us to love parents but to honor them" (LC I 105; K-W, 400–401).

With this commandment, God is assigning a particular "great, good, and holy work" (LC I 112; K-W, 112) to children.[35] Instead of abandoning parents in search of some higher piety as in monasticism, God's Word locates the discipleship of children in their responsibility toward parents:

> For God's sake, therefore, let us finally learn that young
> people should banish all other things from their sight
> and give first place to this commandment. If they wish

---

34  Oswald Bayer, "The Protestant Understanding of Marriage and Family," in *Freedom in Response*, 158.

35  In the words of William Lazareth, "The greatness of Luther's ethical realism lies in his incorporation of this myriad of social interactions into the never-ceasing rule of God," *Luther on the Christian Home* (Philadelphia: Muhlenberg Press, 1960), 132. Lazareth provides an insightful treatment of Luther's understanding of the Fourth Commandment in Chapter 5, "The Common Life" (132–65).

to serve God with truly good works, they must do what is pleasing to their fathers and mothers, or to those to whom they are subject in their stead. For every child who knows and does this has, in the first place, the great comfort of being able joyfully to boast in defiance of all who are occupied with works of their own choice: "See, this work is well-pleasing to my God in heaven; this I know for certain." Let all of them come forward with their many, great, laborious, and difficult works and boast. Let us see whether they can produce a single work that is greater and nobler than obeying father and mother, which God has ordained and commanded next to obedience to his own majesty. If God's Word and will are placed first and are observed, nothing ought to be considered more important than the will and word of our parents, provided that these, too, are subordinated to God and are not set in opposition to the preceding commandments.

(LC I 115–16; K-W, 402)

The Fourth Commandment recognizes the uniqueness of the office of parent in that parents are God's masks for the blessing of children in both the spiritual and temporal realms. This thought is nicely captured by Paul Althaus:

> Parental authority is uniquely different from all other authority because it functions in both governments. Parents not only exercise authority over their children in the secular government, but they also proclaim the gospel to their children. Thus they are at one and the same time secular authorities and, through the universal priesthood, spiritual authorities for their children.[36]

---

36    Paul Althaus, *The Ethics of Martin Luther,* trans. Robert C. Schultz (Philadelphia: Fortress Press, 1972), 99.

In this way, the Fourth Commandment serves as something of a bridge between the Third Commandment and the commandments of the second table that follow. Parents are to be honored, because through them God is both nurturing the life of faith that gives access to the heavenly kingdom and defending children against sin and evil that would destroy bodily life in this world.

Disciples do not pit honor to parents against obedience to God. God hides His majesty behind the mask of mother and father so that to serve and obey them is to serve and obey God. Of course, Luther makes allowance for the fact that parents and others in authority step out of their God-given office and go beyond the commandments of the Creator, demanding that their children and subjects treat them as a substitute god. In this case, God rather than human beings is to be obeyed (see Acts 5:29). The First Commandment always gets the last word.

> **God hides His majesty behind the mask of mother and father so that to serve and obey them is to serve and obey God.**

In the Small Catechism, Luther omits the biblical promise attached to this commandment in Exodus 20:12: "that your days may be long in the land that the LORD your God is giving you." In the Large Catechism, however, Luther notes that experience teaches that the keeping of this commandment yields temporal benefits even as those who break it bring destruction and death on themselves.

In short, the Fourth Commandment is a superb illustration of the doctrine of vocation for Luther. Extending this commandment to include not only biological children but also servants, students, and citizens,[37] Luther writes:

---

37 Here note that Luther identifies three kinds of fathers in this commandment: biological fathers, fathers of households, and political fathers. See LC I 158; K-W, 408.

If this could be impressed on the poor people, a servant girl would dance for joy and praise and thank God; and with her careful work, for which she receives sustenance and wages, she would obtain a treasure such as those who are regarded as the greatest saints do not have. Is it not a tremendous honor to know this and to say, "If you do your daily household chores, that is better than the holiness and austere life of all the monks?" Moreover, you have the promise that whatever you do will prosper and fare well. How could you be more blessed or lead a holier life, as far as works are concerned? In God's sight it is actually faith that makes a person holy; it alone serves God, while our works serve people.

(LC I 145–47; K-W, 406)

Righteous by faith alone, the disciple does not run away from the most mundane and menial aspects of daily life but rather sees the family as the arena where faith is now active in love.

## THE FIFTH COMMANDMENT

Disciples have responsibility for the bodily life of the neighbor. Luther sees in the Fifth Commandment not only the prohibition against the wanton destruction of the neighbor's life but positively the obligation that we "help and support him in every physical need." The fear and love of God above all things is the foundation for both the prohibition of murder and the positive obligation to love the neighbor by providing bodily help and support. "The origin and root of killing do not lie in our hand; they lie in the heart overcome by anger."[38] The love of God is demonstrated by the love for the neighbor, and this love is anything but a wistful

---

38   Peters, *Ten Commandments*, 226.

sentimentality; it is a love turned outward to the real needs of the neighbor in this life. So Luther writes in the Large Catechism,

> This commandment is violated not only when we do evil, but also when we have the opportunity to do good to our neighbors and to prevent, protect, and save them from suffering bodily harm or injury, but fail to do so. If you send a naked person away when you could clothe him, you have let him freeze to death. If you see anyone who is suffering from hunger and do not feed her, you have let her starve. Likewise, if you see anyone who is condemned to death or in similar peril and do not save him although you have means and ways to do so, you have killed him. It will be of no help for you to use the excuse that you did not assist their deaths by word or deed, for you have withheld your love from them and robbed them of the kindness by means of which their lives might have been saved.
>
> (LC I 189–90; K-W, 412)

Luther says that God has erected this commandment in a world that is evil and in the midst of a life that is full of misery.[39] The commandment stands as a protective wall around human life, curbing those who would out of the malice of a renegade heart attack and destroy the life God has given. As with the other commandments, the Fifth Commandment is a concrete expression of the First Commandment: "He always wants to remind us to recall the First Commandment, that he is our God; that is, he wishes to help, comfort, and protect us, so that he may restrain our desire for revenge" (LC I 195; K-W, 413).

Seen through the lens of the First Commandment, the Fifth Commandment turns the heart and hands of the disciple to the neediness of the neighbor's body. Because the body is the place

---

39 "But the occasion and need for this commandment is that, as God well knows, the world is evil and this life is full of misery. Therefore he has erected this and the other commandments to separate good and evil" (LC I 183; K-W, 411).

of the neighbor's life, it is not killed, either directly by assault or indirectly by withholding that which is necessary to sustain life. Instead, it is the way of discipleship to care for the body of the neighbor, providing food to the hungry, medical aid to the sick, hospitality to the homeless, and protection to those whose physical life is threatened by violence. Here again, the positive aspect of the commandment is open ended and not restricted by the boundaries of ethical limitation implied in the lawyer's question to Jesus in Luke 10:29: "Who is my neighbor?"

## THE SIXTH COMMANDMENT

Discipleship is not antithetical to marriage. The Creator who made humanity in His image as male and female, giving Adam and Eve to each other and blessing their one-flesh union by making it procreative, instituted marriage prior to the fall into sin. "Marriage is a *benedictio* of God. As God's work, commandment, and blessing, marriage is a divine estate, through which the reflection of God's good creation still shines."[40] The Sixth Commandment is God's protective wall around marriage, guarding the lives of those who are now one flesh, sustaining it in the face of the world's attacks, the devil's deceptions, and the lust of the flesh. Luther captures this thought in the Large Catechism: "Thus God wants to guard and protect every husband or wife through this commandment against anyone who would violate them" (LC I 205; K-W, 414).

Luther's explanation of the Sixth Commandment, unlike the other commandments, is stated entirely in the positive: "We should fear and love God so that we lead a sexually pure and decent life in what we say and do, and husband and wife love and honor each other." It is this positive assertion that forms the basis in the Large Catechism for Luther's explicit admonitions to avoid all

---

40  Peters, *Ten Commandments*, 249.

forms of sexual impurity. Luther sees marriage as foundational for human life:

> He has established it before all others as the first of all institutions, and he created man and woman differently (as is evident) not for indecency but to be true to each other, to be fruitful, to beget children, and to nurture and bring them up to the glory of God.
>
> (LC I 207; K-W, 414)[41]

To protect marriage as an honorable and God-pleasing way of life, God forbids both outward acts of fornication and marital unfaithfulness, as well as the chaotic lusts of the heart.

Echoing the apostle's exhortation that believers are to "abstain from sexual immorality" (1 Thessalonians 4:3; see also Ephesians 5:3; Colossians 3:5; Galatians 5:19; 1 Corinthians 6:16–20), the Reformer writes,

> But inasmuch as there is such a shameless mess and cesspool of all sorts of immorality and indecency among us, this commandment is also directly against every form of unchastity, no matter what it is called. Not only is the outward act forbidden, but also every kind of cause, provocation, and means, so that your heart, your lips, and your entire body may be chaste and afford no occasion, aid, or encouragement to unchastity.
>
> (LC I 202; K-W, 414)[42]

Luther observes that God instituted marriage as the appropriate channel for sexual desire, noting that "where nature[43] functions

---

41    Here note Paul Althaus: "Thus marriage is both God's original intention for his creation before all sin and the means by which he now uses it to protect people against the destructive power of unrestrained sexuality," *The Ethics of Martin Luther*, 85.

42    Werner Elert notes the connection of the Sixth Commandment to the First Commandment in his observation that "Paul pointed out that sexual immorality comes as a consequence of atheism," *The Christian Ethos*, 92. Also Hans Walter Wolff: "The uniqueness of Yahweh's love relationship to Israel meant a fundamental prohibition of adultery (Ex. 20:3, 14)," in *Anthropology of the Old Testament*, 173.

43    Bayer, "Luther's View of Marriage," in *Freedom in Response*, 173. As an estate ordained by God, marriage has

as God implanted it, however, it is not possible to remain chaste outside of marriage; for flesh and blood remain flesh and blood, and natural inclinations and stimulations proceed unrestrained and unimpeded, as everyone observes and experiences" (LC I 212; K-W, 415). Genuine celibacy is rare, says Luther, "a high, super-natural gift" (LC I 211; K-W, 415).

In seeking after a higher form of discipleship in claiming celibacy as a more God-pleasing way of life, spiritually more significant than marriage, priests, monks, and nuns often fell into greater sin as they were incapable of keeping their vows. While marriage is not a sacrament, Luther sees no higher form of human life than marriage. It is a way of life blessed by God, where husband and wife love and honor each other and serve the world in bearing and rearing children. In short, marriage is the venue for discipleship under the cross.

The liturgical order for Luther's marriage rite reminds the congregation that marriage is *sub crucis,* under the cross: "hear also the cross that God has placed upon this estate" (Marriage Booklet 14; K-W, 370). The language of the cross in relation to marriage was retained in Lutheran marriage liturgies until the late-twentieth century. It is a shame that the reference to the cross in marriage was deleted in our more recent liturgical agendas. The cross comes with the territory of marriage as it does with all callings in this world.[44]

Men and women who are disciples of Jesus Christ enter into marriage, confessing it an estate instituted and sustained by the Word of the Creator. In the words of Oswald Bayer, "We cannot see our marriage simply as brought about by own decision or

---

permanence and durability. Here also note Bayer: "In the light of all this, we can understand why Luther placed so much emphasis on the 'estate' of marriage. For us this has become an old-fashioned word that suggests something solid and immovable. But for Luther the concept of estate was intimately connected with both steadfastness and energy, products of the reliability of the Word that ensures that life together will have the quality of endurance. The Word holds all the various facets of an active life together, its beauty and peace as well as its crises and conflicts. The Word of God lends stability to the estate of marriage and brings about unconditional and permanent unity of one man and one woman" (170).

44   Here see the discussion of the relationship of cross and vocation in Gustaf Wingren, *Luther on Vocation,* trans. Carl C. Rasmussen (Philadelphia: Muhlenberg Press, 1957), 50ff. Especially Wingren's observation that "The cross is not to be chosen by us; it is laid upon us by God, i.e., the cross comes uninvoked in our vocation" (53).

just a contract that can be dissolved by mutual consent." Yoked together under the cross, husband and wife live together as one flesh, trusting in the promises of Christ Jesus and clinging to each other in love.

# The Seventh Commandment

Generosity, not greed, characterizes the life of discipleship. The Seventh Commandment protects the earthly gifts that God has given to our neighbors. We are forbidden to take the neighbor's money or property through outright theft or crafty acts of dishonesty. Instead, disciples invest themselves in the well-being of the neighbors, assisting them in protecting and promoting their livelihood. "Our help is not to confirm and leave our fellow man in beggary and laziness but to get him out of there and place him on his own two feet."[45]

The opposite of theft is vocation. "Let the thief no longer steal, but rather let him labor, doing honest work with his own hands, so that he may have something to share with anyone in need" (Ephesians 4:28). God has arranged the world economically so that human beings are both givers and receivers. God uses other people in their various callings as the "masks" behind which He hides to give us creaturely gifts to sustain us in this life. We in turn are the "masks" behind which the Creator operates to give these good gifts to others.

Stealing is taking in place of giving. It deprives the neighbor of the good things that God has given him. The thief is at one and the same time engaged in an act of idolatry, for in his robbery of the neighbor, he launches an assault on the God who is the Giver of every good and perfect gift. In depriving the neighbor of property, goods, or money, the thief is robbing God. Such is not the way of discipleship.

---

45   Peters, *Ten Commandments*, 265.

Enlivened by faith in the unending generosity of the triune God, who is the donor of all that we have, disciples' lives are turned outward to serve the neighbor with their good works. Luther concludes his treatment of the Seventh Commandment in the Large Catechism:

> Anyone who seeks and desires good works will find here more than enough things to do that are heartily acceptable and pleasing to God. Moreover, God lavishes upon them a wonderful blessing, and generously rewards us for what we do to benefit and befriend our neighbor, as King Solomon also teaches in Proverbs 19[:17]: "Whoever is kind to the poor lends to the LORD, and will be repaid in full." Here you have a rich Lord, who is surely sufficient for your needs and will let you lack or want for nothing. Thus with a happy conscience you can enjoy a hundred times more than you could scrape together by perfidy and injustice. Whoever does not desire this blessing will find wrath and misfortune enough.
>
> (LC I 252–53; K-W, 420)

## THE EIGHTH COMMANDMENT

Luther writes, "Besides our own body, our spouse, and our temporal property, we have one more treasure that is indispensable to us, namely, our honor and good reputation. For it is important that we do not live among people in public disgrace and dishonor" (LC I 255; K-W, 420). The Eighth Commandment has to do with the lips of the disciple as God protects reputations by forbidding false testimony, lies about the neighbor. "It not only prohibits lying assertions about the neighbor, but it even prohibits us from dragging the secret sins of the neighbor into the light and discussing them with others."[46]

Bound by the law of love, disciples live with guarded lips, not only putting away every form of falsehood but also being careful not to use the truth in a way that shames the neighbor or harms his character. The tongue, James says, can be a force of destruction (see James 3:6–11), incapable of being tamed. The tongue of the disciple is intended for blessing and confession, not for cursing and lying.

# The Ninth and Tenth Commandments

The Ninth and Tenth Commandments address the desires of the heart as they forbid coveting, which is a manifestation of idolatry. In this way, they lead the disciple back to the First Commandment.[47] God prevents the greedy heart from devising schemes to confiscate the people and things that God has given to the neighbor. When the heart reaches for what God has not given, it is not fearing, loving, and trusting in the God who is our Father and Creator. It is sin to take for ourselves what God has not bestowed. "As our Creator and Redeemer, God does not want us to get bogged down in this perishing world of death and idolize what is perishable."[48]

The flip side of covetousness is contentment. Content with the people and possessions that God has given, the life of the disciple is turned outward toward serving the neighbor and helping him keep what God has given. Rather than enticing spouse, employees,

---

46   Peters, *Ten Commandments*, 287.

47   Here also note Peters: "The instruction 'Do not covet' not only summarizes, according to Rom. 13:9, the last two commandments, but according to Rom. 7:7, it also summarizes the entire Decalogue, even the entire Law" (*Ten Commandments*, 310). Ernst Käsemann observes, "Sin, here defined as the power and the reality of covetousness, is both stimulated and unmasked by the law of the divine commandment," in *Commentary on Romans*, trans. G. W. Bromiley (Grand Rapids: Eerdmans, 1980), 193.

48   Peters, *Ten Commandments*, 310. Also note Peters' characterization of the way in which coveting is an expression of original sin: "This egotistic thirst for life, this greedy clinging to the earth, this natural referring everything to oneself—we are born into it, we have inherited it without our will and collaboration, but we have accepted it in the core of our existence" (*Ten Commandments*, 313).

or even animals away from our neighbors, we are to "urge them to stay and do their duty."

The final two commandments of the Decalogue accuse us, showing forth the guilt of hearts that lust after that which has been given to the neighbor but not to us. Beyond these two commandments are the Creed and the Lord's Prayer. The Creed is the catalog and summary of all that the triune God has given in creation, redemption, and sanctification for body and soul. Covetousness would blind our eyes to the bounty and generosity of the God who in Christ freely gives us all things. The First Article expands our vision, opening our eyes to the fact that God has created me, given me all that I have, and still preserves my life in this world. The Second Article confesses my redemption as a lost and condemned person by the Passion of Christ so that I might be His own and live under Him in His kingdom. The Third Article narrates how the Holy Spirit has called me by the Gospel—daily and richly forgiving me my sins—and will at the end bring me to the resurrection of the body and life everlasting. In this divine economy, I lack nothing that is good. The Lord's Prayer teaches us to pray for all that God has commanded and promised in the confidence that the heavenly Father gives daily bread, that is, all that I need for this body and life, and that finally He will deliver me from every evil of body and soul and give to His disciples the gift of heaven itself.

# THE CONCLUSION

The Small Catechism's Conclusion to the Decalogue takes us back the First Commandment, and in this way brings all of the Commandments back to their source and center.[49] God threatens

---

49   "Thus the First Commandment is to illuminate and impart its splendor to all the others. In order that this may be constantly repeated and never forgotten, therefore, you must let these concluding words run through all the commandments, like the clasp or hoop of a wreath that binds the end to the beginning and holds everything together. ...Thus you see how the First Commandment is the chief source and fountainhead that permeates all others; again, to it they all return and upon it they depend, so that end and beginning are completely linked and bound together" (LC I 326, 329; K-W, 430). Commenting on how the First Commandment is "the chief source and fountainhead," Schlink

punishment to all who break these Commandments, while promising grace and every blessing to all who keep them. The Ten Commandments hold out the promise of a blessed life to all who keep them, but they are powerless to enable sinners to keep them. Good and wise though they are, to use the language of Matthias Loy's hymn, the Decalogue will not and cannot save:

> The Law is good; but since the fall
> Its holiness condemns us all;
> It dooms us for our sin to die
> And has no pow'r to justify.

(LSB 579:5)

Disciples know that "Christ is the end of the law for righteousness to everyone who believes" (Romans 10:4). Freed from the curse of the Law in the conscience, the

> **"Christ is the end of the law for righteousness to everyone who believes" (Romans 10:4).**

Law is not dismissed but instead takes its place in creation, putting to death the old Adam's attempts to create his own good works before God and instead focusing our attention on the works God has declared to be good. So the Ten Commandments remain in the life of discipleship not as a path to salvation but as the concrete way that those who fear, love, and trust in God above all things now live in His world, giving themselves to the service and well-being of their neighbor.

> Here, then, we have the Ten Commandments, a summary of divine teaching on what we are to do to make our whole life pleasing to God. They are the true fountain from which all good works must spring, the true channel through which all good works must flow. Apart from these Ten Commandments no action or

---

observes, "Thus we love God only when we 'fear, love, and trust in God above all things.' This love is demanded as obedience to the concrete commandments of both tables" (*Theology of the Lutheran Confessions*), 74.

life can be good or pleasing to God, no matter how great or precious it may be in the eyes of the world.

(LC I 311; K-W, 428)

The life of the disciple is given to the continuous learning and practice of the Ten Commandments in this old and dying world, even as we live by faith in the crucified and risen Lord, who has fulfilled the Law for us. Luther gives this advice in his 1520 *Treatise on Good Works*:

> There is just no better mirror in which to see your need than the Ten Commandments, in which you will find what you lack and what you should seek. Therefore, where you find in yourself a weak faith, feeble hope, and little love toward God; where you find that you do not praise and honor God but love your own honor and fame, think much of the favor of men, do not gladly hear mass and sermon, are too lazy to pray (in which matters there is no one who has not sinned), then you must pay more heed to these infirmities than to all physical harm to goods, honor, and life, and believe that they are worse than death and all mortal sickness. You should earnestly lay these [infirmities] before God, lament and ask for help, and with all confidence expect help, believing that you are heard and that you will receive help and mercy.

(AE 44:63)

The path of discipleship avoids both the ditches of legalism ("lawfulness") and antinomianism ("lawlessness"). Only where the Law is rightly distinguished from the Gospel will the Ten Commandments be guarded against both of these abuses. It is only when this distinction is rightly made that the Decalogue can be embraced not as a path to salvation but as the path that the disciple walks within this fallen creation, fearing, loving, and trusting the triune God above all things and serving the neighbor in love according to the will of our Creator.

*FOR FURTHER REFLECTION AND STUDY: CONNECTIONS WITH LUTHER'S SMALL CATECHISM WITH EXPLANATION 2017*

1. Read Luke 12:13–34. How is the First Commandment working in this text?

2. Whatever we "fear, love, and trust" in above all things is our god. How do false gods finally fail?

3. What sets Christian faith apart from all other religions? (See pp. 65–66.)

4. How do we know God's name? (See pp. 67–68.) How are we to use His name? (See pp. 69–71.)

5. What is God's purpose in the Third Commandment? (See pp. 75–76.)

6. How do disciples worship the triune God? (See pp. 78–80; see also "What Is Worship?" on pp. 358–59.)

7. How are disciples to honor, serve, obey, love, and cherish their parents? (See pp. 81–83.)

8. How does the Fifth Commandment both prohibit murder and prescribe care for the neighbor in his or her bodily life? (See pp. 85–87.)

9. What is marriage? (See pp. 93–97.) How are disciples to live within marriage? (See pp. 98–104.)

10. What does the Seventh Commandment say about a disciple's use of property? (See pp. 105–7.)

11. How does the Eighth Commandment govern the disciple's use of language? (See pp. 110–12.)

12. What is coveting? How is it an expression of idolatry? (See pp. 115–18.)

13. How does "The Close of the Commandments" take disciples back to the First Commandment? (See pp. 120–22.)

## Chapter 3

The Creed: Disciples Confess the Faith

> These are the three persons and one God, who has
> given himself to us all wholly and completely, with
> all that he is and has. The Father gives himself to us,
> with heaven and earth and all the creatures, in order
> that they may serve us and benefit us. But this gift
> has become obscured and useless through Adam's fall.
> Therefore the Son himself subsequently gave himself
> and bestowed all his works, sufferings, wisdom, and
> righteousness, and reconciled us to the Father, in order
> that restored to life and righteousness, we might also
> know and have the Father and his gifts.
>
> MARTIN LUTHER, *CONFESSION CONCERNING CHRIST'S SUPPER*
> *(1528)* (AE 37:366)

Disciples are those who hear God's Word and say back to God what He has said to us. This is confession of faith. What is believed in the heart is confessed with the lips (Romans 10:9–11) in the presence of God and the world. Disciples are not given to talk about their faith but about the saving God who is faith's object: Father, Son, and Holy Spirit. The Apostles' Creed is the "everyday" creed for disciples. This creed is the summation of the trinitarian name into which we

**This creed is the summation of the trinitarian name into which we are baptized and now live.**

are baptized and now live. Luther envisions Christians confessing the Apostles' Creed at the beginning and end of each day as it puts us in mind of our Baptism, in the name of the Father and of the Son and of the Holy Spirit.[50]

Luther did not see the Trinity as a problem to be solved or a mystery to be unraveled but as the truth of God's revelation of Himself to be proclaimed and confessed.[51] Writing late in his life (1543), in the treatise on *The Last Words of David*, Luther takes up the doctrine of the Trinity:

> **Thus it is useful and proper that there be some, both among the laity and the educated, particularly pastors, preachers, schoolmasters, who think it important to learn about such centrally important articles of our faith and to speak of them in German. . . . But for the one for whom this is too difficult, that person should stay with the children by using the catechism and should pray against the devil and his nonsense.[52]**

Neither the Small or Large Catechism provide a dogmatic discussion of the Trinity. Instead, Luther assumes the biblical and creedal truth of doctrine and proceeds to confess and teach not on the basis of abstractions but on God's revelation of Himself in Christ.

To confess that God is Creator is the simplest way of describing who God is, according to the Large Catechism. God is the Father who made heaven and earth, "for there is no one else who could create heaven and earth" (LC II 11; K-W, 432). Nothing has

---

50   The observation of Carl Beckwith is on target: "For Luther, Christian salvation, identity, and ethics find their coherence and grammar in the Trinity and our trinitarian confession. We live in Christ by the Holy Spirit to the delight of the Father," in *Confessional Lutheran Dogmatics*, vol. 3: *The Holy Trinity* (Fort Wayne, The Luther Academy, 2016), 5.

51   For more on Luther on the Trinity, see Christine Helmer, *The Trinity and Martin Luther* (Bellingham, WA: Lexham Press, 2017); Steven Paulson, "Luther's Doctrine of God," in *The Oxford Handbook of Martin Luther's Theology*, ed. Robert Kolb, Irene Dingel, L'ubomí Baatka (New York: Oxford University Press, 2014), 187–200; and Hans Schwarz, *The Trinity: The Central Mystery of Christianity* (Minneapolis: Fortress Press, 2017), 91–93.

52   Cited in Peters, *Commentary on Luther's Catechisms: Creed*, trans. Thomas H. Trapp (St. Louis: Concordia Publishing House, 2011), 36.

existence apart from Him. To speak of creation presupposes that there is a Creator.

God gives Himself to us completely. Creation, redemption, and faith are all from the triune God. The Catechism echoes the apostle Paul: "What do you have that you did not receive? If then you received it, why do you boast as if you did not receive it?" (1 Corinthians 4:7). Disciples know themselves as creatures of the God and Father of our Lord Jesus Christ, who has not only created them but is also with them in all things. Brought to faith in the Son through the Spirit's work in the Gospel, disciples now see creation as a gift received purely out of God's "fatherly, divine goodness and mercy, without any merit or worthiness in me." In the words of Oswald Bayer, this means that everything God does for us is "categorical gift."[53] We can take no credit for God's creating, redeeming, and sanctifying us.[54] The action of the verbs in Luther's explanation of the Apostles' Creed are done by God, not by human beings. "For here we see how the Father has given to us himself with all creation and has abundantly provided for us in this life, apart from the fact that he has also showered us with inexpressible eternal blessings through his Son and the Holy Spirit" (LC II 24; K-W, 433). The shape of God's giving is trinitarian as the Father gives us all things in His Son through the Holy Spirit. The Father wills salvation. The Son accomplishes salvation. The Holy Spirit delivers salvation through the external word of the Gospel.[55]

> **The shape of God's giving is trinitarian as the Father gives us all things in His Son through the Holy Spirit.**

---

53 Here see Oswald Bayer, "Categorical Imperative or Categorical Gift?" in *Freedom in Response*, 13–20; and "The Ethics of Gift," *Lutheran Quarterly* 24 (2010): 447–68.

54 Again see Bayer: "If the Son and the Spirit justify the unrighteous without any merit of worthiness on their part (Rom. 4:5), then the creative activity of the Father takes place, and rightly so, 'without any merit or worthiness on my part,'" in "I Believe That God Has Created Me with All That Exists: An Example of Catechetical-Systematics," *Lutheran Quarterly* 8, no. 2 (1994): 336.

55 This is beautifully expressed in stanza 7 of the Reformation-era hymn by Ludwig Helmbold, "From God Can Nothing Move Me," where the hymnist confesses: "For thus the Father willed it, Who fashioned us from clay; And His own Son fulfilled it And brought eternal day. The Spirit now has come, To us true faith has given; He leads us home

# THE FIRST ARTICLE:

The stance of the disciple is receptivity. Luther describes the totality of the Father's giving in the Large Catechism:

> Moreover, we also confess that God the Father has given us not only all that we have and what we see before our eyes, but also that he daily guards and defends us against every evil and misfortune, warding off all sorts of danger and disaster. All this he does out of pure love and goodness, without our merit, as a kind father who cares for us so that no evil may befall us. . . . Hence, because everything we possess, and everything in heaven and on earth besides, is daily given, sustained, and protected by God, it inevitably follows that we are in duty bound to love, praise, and thank him without ceasing, and, in short, devote all these things to his service, as he has required and enjoined in the Ten Commandments.
>
> (LC II 17–19; K-W, 433)

Having received all things from God, we now become active as masks, instruments, and channels of God's work in creation. Because the Father has given us His Son, we see creation with new eyes. Writing on John's Gospel, Luther says,

> Now if I believe in God's Son and bear in mind that He became man, all creatures will appear a hundred times more beautiful to me than before. Then I will properly appreciate the sun, the moon, the stars, trees, apples, and pears, as I reflect that He is Lord over all and the Center of all things.
>
> (AE 22:496)[56]

---

to heaven. O praise the Three in One" (*LSB* 713:7; © 2006 CPH).

56    For a helpful overview of Luther's appreciation of the natural world, see "The Picture of Nature," in Heinrich

Without Christ, creation is seen as a threat to be mastered, matter to be manipulated by the human will, or as the object of entitlement.[57] Knowing the truth of Christ, creation is received as a gift, not an idol to be worshiped or a danger to be avoided.

Disciples "practice" the First Article as it opens their eyes to apprehend the world God has made:

> **For this reason we ought daily to practice this article, impress it upon our minds, and remember it in everything we see and in every blessing that comes our way. Whenever we escape distress or danger, we should recognize how God gives and does all of this so that we may sense and see in them his fatherly heart and his boundless love toward us. Thus our hearts will be warmed and kindled with gratitude to God and a desire to use all these blessings to his glory and praise.**
>
> (LC II 23; K-W, 433)

The confession of the First Article is inclusive of both cosmological breadth and personal specificity: "God has made me and all creatures."[58] We know from Genesis 1–2 that God created the heavens and the earth in the beginning. The Lord God who brought all things into existence, creating time itself and setting the work of His hands in order within the first six days, now continues His creative work. Here Luther gets personal as he confesses, God "has made me." The God who created Adam and Eve at this world's beginning has also made me. Luther does not, however, dissolve God's original creation into His ongoing

---

Bornkamm, *Luther's World of Thought*, trans. Martin Bertram (St. Louis: Concordia Publishing House, 1958), 176–94.

57    Here note Luther's comment in his lectures on Genesis 43: "Things that are most pleasant and agreeable by their own nature it [the terrified conscience] turns into wormwood and gall. Indeed, the whole creation, created for the use and pleasure of men, seems hostile and to threaten pestilence and destruction" (AE 7:322).

58    Werner Elert writes of Luther's confession in the First Article: "He has made me and all creatures": "God has not created me as one who is isolated; He has created me as a creature in sum total of all. Here faith in my Creator has become a hymn of praise to the preservation of my environment and of the world in general. Luther cannot separate either God or himself from the natural environment," in *The Structure of Lutheranism*, 449.

creation.[59] Rather, God's creative work in the beginning is the foundation for His ongoing preservation of creation, as through His creatures, He continues to create and sustain.[60] We are not "co-creators" with God, who alone is the almighty Father, maker of heaven and earth, but we do cooperate with Him in the sense that He uses us as His masks, that is, as the tools, instruments, and channels of His ongoing work in creation.[61]

God is the giver of "my body and soul, eyes, ears, and all my members, my reason and all my senses." The human being is an embodied soul possessing physical members ("eyes, ears, and all my members") as well as the capacities for thought, reflection, and sensation. The human body in all of its dimensions both externally and internally is God's craftsmanship (see Psalm 139:13–16). Echoing Psalm 100, Luther confesses that it is God who has made us, and we are His, even as Luther accents the reality of God's continued providential care for the human life He has created.

The Creator takes care of His human creatures through creation. Luther catalogs the gifts God gives to support this body and life: "clothing and shoes, food and drink, house and home, wife and children, land, animals, and all I have." Here Luther sets the personal within the communal as the benefactions God "richly and daily provides me" come in and through other creatures. The life of the disciple is not that of an individual alone before God, drawn out of creation, but is set within creation, where he or she continues to receive all good things from the Father's generosity through His created instruments. Here Luther's explanation of the First Article bears striking resemblance to the Fourth Petition

---

59    Here see the helpful article by Johannes Schwanke, "Doctrine of Creation," in *The Oxford Encyclopedia of Martin Luther*, vol. 1, edited by Derek R. Nelson and Paul R. Hinlicky (New York: Oxford University Press, 2017), 366–83. Schwanke writes, "Luther's holding on to a historic Paradise, a historic Adam and historic Fall may seem odd to contemporary science-oriented Christians, but for Luther all three are necessary because of theological reasons. The *creatio prima* or *creatio originans* must not be dissolved into the *creatio continua*" (370).

60    For example, in his lectures on Genesis 2:2, Luther writes, "The Word which He spoke in the beginning is still in existence, as Ps. 33:9 says: 'He spoke, and it came into being'" (AE 1:76).

61    "Just as God uses all creatures as his hands, channels, and means through which to bless human beings, the recipients of these blessings are to be the hands, channels, and means by which God blesses others," in William Weinrich, "Creation," in *Confessing the Gospel Today: A Lutheran Approach to Systematic Theology*, vol. 1, ed. Samuel Nafzger et al. (St. Louis: Concordia Publishing House, 2017), 159.

of the Lord's Prayer, where Jesus teaches His disciples to pray for "daily bread."[62]

There is nothing idyllic about Luther's confession of the First Article as he recognizes that fallen creation is a tragic place, where the bodily life given by God is imperiled. Hence he asserts that God defends me against all danger and guards and protects me from all evil. God uses His servants—both angelic and human—to curb the effects of evil in the world. God dispatches His angels to fight for us and defend us in ways beyond our knowledge (see Psalm 91). He uses those who occupy earthly offices of authority and service, whether they be parents, police, soldiers, medical workers, and the like to guard and protect us from harm.

> **He recognizes that fallen creation is a tragic place, where the bodily life given by God is imperiled.**

Creation is not done out of necessity but out of the Father's goodwill to express His "fatherly, divine goodness and mercy, without any merit or worthiness in me." Luther invites Peter, his Wittenberg barber, to meditate on this article of the Creed:

> You are God's creation, his handiwork, his workmanship. That is, of yourself and in yourself you are nothing, can do nothing, know nothing, are capable of nothing. What were you a thousand years ago? What were heaven and earth six thousand years ago? Nothing, just as that which will never be created is nothing. But what you are, know, can do, and can achieve is God's creation, as you confess [in the Creed] by word of mouth.
>
> (AE 43:210)

---

62    Here note Bayer: "Luther does not lose himself in the abundance of what he has listed but frames and assimilates these nouns under the aspect of the radical impossibility of the world's autonomy that includes my life in this world," in "I Believe That God Has Created Me," 129. The nouns of both Luther's explanation of the First Article and the Fourth Petition are gifts but also necessities for life, and they are not self-generated.

God's gifts in creation are neither deserved nor merited; they are benefactions bestowed out of a Father's heart of love, mercy, and kindness.

Disciples recognize and confess creation as the gift of a good and gracious Father. It is not to be abused, ignored, or despised, but received in faith. We are not drawn out of creation to live in some spiritualistic sphere, but we remain in this world to live as creatures who look to the Creator for every good. Creation becomes the arena where disciples now have their duty "to thank and praise, serve and obey" God.[63] The disciples' confession of the First Article is essentially to praise God, to recognize God as the Father, the almighty maker of heaven and earth. Without such praise, Hans Walter Wolff observes that man "becomes his own idol, turns into a tyrant; either that, or falling dumb, he loses his freedom."[64]

## The Second Article

Disciples belong to the Lord, who has made them His own. Luther's explanation of the Second Article of the Apostles' Creed answers two fundamental questions: Who is this Lord? What has He done? For Luther, Christology (the doctrine of Christ's person) and soteriology (the doctrine of Christ's work) are of one fabric.[65]

> Through the Gospel we are told who Christ is, in order
> that we may learn to know that He is our Savior, that
> He delivers us from sin and death, helps us out of all

---

63  Peters observes, "The commandment thus grows immediately out of God's giving of Himself to us; as the '*usus practicus Evangelii*,' it carries the gracious act of Christ secretly within it already," *Creed*, 102. Also note the observation of Charles Arand: "Without a robust theology of creation, the teaching of redemption would become unmoored and float away into a spiritualistic realm of escape," in "The Unbounded Creator and the Bounded Creature," *Lutheran Quarterly* 31 (Autumn 2017): 267.

64  Hans Walter Wolff, *Anthropology of the Old Testament*, trans. Margaret Kohl (Philadelphia: Fortress Press, 1974), 229.

65  "The work of Jesus Christ would be worthless for us if he were not God's Son and as such very God, and our faith would be merely a new work of self-righteousness if in it God's Spirit and therefore God himself were not active, by whose power alone we can lay hold of the work of Christ. We have a gracious God as the triune God, or we have no gracious God," Edmund Schlink, *Theology of the Lutheran Confessions*, 65. Luther's confession of Christ's person and office are clearly set within the framework of the trinitarian structure of the Creed in the Small Catechism.

misfortune, reconciles us to the Father, and makes us pious and saves us without our works. He who does not learn to know Christ in this way must go wrong. For even though you know that He is God's Son, that He died and rose again, and that He sits at the right hand of the Father, you have not yet learned to know Christ aright, and this knowledge still does not help you. You must also know and believe that He did all this for your sake, in order to help you. Consequently, all that has hitherto been preached and taught at the schools of higher learning is sheer rubbish. They had no understanding of this, and they never went beyond the thought that Christ suffered intensely and that He is now sitting in heaven above with nothing to do and is enjoying Himself. Thus their hearts remain barren, and faith cannot come to life in them. The Lord Christ should not be isolated as existing for Himself but should be preached as belonging to us.

(AE 30:29–30)

Saving knowledge of Christ entails both His person and His work. These come together in the confession that He is "my Lord."[66]

With precision and clarity, Luther puts the ancient definition of "the two natures of Christ" into straightforward language. Of Jesus, Luther says in his sermons on John, "Whoever encounters this flesh encounters God" (AE 23:126). Jesus Christ is "true God, begotten of the Father from eternity, and also true man, born of the Virgin Mary." Begotten of His Father from eternity (see John 1:1–14; 1 Corinthians 8:6; and Colossians 1:16–17).

---

66    Hermann Sasse provides a compelling discussion of Jesus' lordship in his 1931 essay "Jesus Is Lord: The Church's Original Confession," in *We Confess Jesus Christ*, trans. Norman E. Nagel (St. Louis: Concordia Publishing House, 1984), 9–35. Sasse notes, "With the confession that Jesus is *kyrios* the Christian faith is marked off from all surrounding religions. The confession that Jesus is the Christ may have been possible among the Jews. At least the early church thought so, though not the rulers of the Jews (John 9:22). But the confession that Jesus is Lord brought the inseparable separation of synagogue and church. What was seen on the one hand as the deification of a creature and blasphemy against the one and only God was seen on the other as no infringement at all of the fact that there is but one God" (12). To say that Jesus is Lord is to say that this man of Nazareth is Yahweh.

Luther echoes both the New Testament and the ecumenical creeds as he confesses without qualification that Jesus is God.[67] From his conception in Mary's virginal womb, He takes on human flesh and is true man, our brother. Stanza 6 of Luther's hymn "Dear Christians, One and All Rejoice" nicely parallels his catechetical treatment of the Second Article:

> The Son obeyed His Father's will,
> Was born of virgin mother;
> And God's good pleasure to fulfill,
> He came to be my brother.
> His royal pow'r disguised He bore;
> A servant's form, like mine, He wore
> To lead the devil captive.
>
> (*LSB* 556:6)

Luther centers his unfolding of the Second Article on the truth that Jesus Christ, true God and true man, has made Himself "my Lord." To confess that Jesus is "my Lord" is to essentially declare that the Father's eternal Son, conceived by the Holy Spirit and born of Mary, is my Redeemer. This is how Luther expresses it in the Large Catechism:

> **"I believe that Jesus Christ, true Son of God, has become my Lord." What is it "to become a lord"? It means that he has redeemed and released me from sin, from the devil, from death, and from all misfortune. Before this I had no lord or king, but was captive under the power of the devil. I was condemned to death and entangled in sin and blindness.**
>
> (LC II 27; K-W, 434)

The human being never lives in neutrality; he or she will be possessed by something. Without the true Lord Christ Jesus, there

---

67    Here note Ian Siggins: "Without question, Luther holds the assertion of Christ's divinity to be integral to the gospel," in *Martin Luther's Doctrine of Christ* (New Haven: Yale University Press, 1970), 191.

is only bondage to sin, captivity to the devil, and the condemnation of death. Luther vividly portrays the futility of such existence, linking the First Article to his confession of the Second Article:

> For when we were created by God the Father and had received from him all kinds of good things, the devil came and led us into disobedience, sin, death, and all misfortune. As a result, we lay under God's wrath and displeasure, sentenced to eternal damnation, as we had merited it and deserved it.
>
> (LC II 28; K-W, 434)

In contrast to the generosity of the Father in the First Article giving us every good thing out of His "fatherly, divine goodness, and mercy, without any merit or worthiness in me," humanity now merits only God's wrath and condemnation. Again, Luther's language in the Small Catechism brings to mind the words of his great hymn on justification:

> Fast bound in Satan's chains I lay;
>   Death brooded darkly o'er me.
> Sin was my torment night and day;
>   In sin my mother bore me.
> But daily deeper still I fell;
> My life became a living hell,
>   So firmly sin possessed me.
>
> (*LSB* 556:2)

Jesus Christ is the Lord who "purchases and wins" us from the enslavement and despair brought about by sin, which consigns us to the power of the evil one and guarantees a destiny to eternal death. Luther continues in the Large Catechism:

> There was no counsel, no help, no comfort for us until this only and eternal Son of God, in his unfathomable goodness, had mercy on us because of our misery and distress and came from heaven to help us. Those tyrants

and jailers have now been routed, and their place has been taken by Jesus Christ, the Lord of life, righteousness, and every good and blessing. He has snatched us, poor lost creatures, from the jaws of hell, won us, made us free, and restored us to the Father's favor and grace. As his own possession he has taken us under his protection and shelter, in order that he may rule us by his righteousness, wisdom, power, life, and blessedness.

(LC II 29–30; K-W, 434)[68]

The focus here is on Christ for us. In 1521, a few years before writing the Small Catechism, the Reformer penned a short booklet entitled *A Brief Instruction on What to Look for and Expect in the Gospels*. In this catechetical tract, Luther warned his readers against making Christ into a new Moses, that is, in seeing Him simply as an example for godly living. Instead, Luther said, "You must grasp Christ at a much higher level. . . . The chief article and foundation of the gospel is that before you take Christ as an example, you accept and recognize him as a gift, as a present that God has given you and that is your own" (AE 35:119).[69] This is precisely how Luther is preaching Christ in his explanation of the Creed. The Gospel is the narration of Christ's story; who He is and what He has done to rescue and redeem sinners. However, it is more than a lesson in biblical history; it is a story with a

---

68    Here also see Marc Lienhard: "Lost human beings, separated from God by the abyss of sin, subject to the divine wrath, enslaved to sin, the law, and death, are faced by the love of God, who has sent the Son. He came to share our conditions of existence; the innocent became one with sinners; he offered himself to the wrath of the Father and bore our punishment for sin; he triumphed over the law, the devil, and death. Coming to us when the gospel is proclaimed, he offers himself to faith as the righteousness we present before God, he triumphs over the powers who enslave us and he renders us in conformity with his resurrection," in *Luther: Witness to Jesus Christ*, trans. Edwin H. Robinson (Minneapolis: Augsburg Publishing House, 1982), 371. In this way, to use the words of the Catechism, Christ has "made me His own."

69    In a similar fashion in his 1522 "Prefaces to the New Testament," Luther provides this stunning definition of the Gospel: "See to it, therefore, that you do not make a Moses out of Christ, or a book of laws and doctrines out of the gospel, as has been done heretofore and as certain prefaces put it, even those of St. Jerome. For the gospel does not expressly demand works of our own by which we become righteous and are saved; indeed it condemns such works. Rather the gospel demands faith in Christ: that he has overcome for us sin, death, and hell, and thus gives us righteousness, life, and salvation not through our works, but through his own works, death, and suffering, in order that we may avail ourselves of his death and victory as though we had done it ourselves" (AE 35:360).

promise attached. This Christ is for me. He has redeemed me. Steven Paulson aptly captures Luther's point:

> Promises from Christ mean nothing in general, they must have the subject, for you, with them or they are worse than nothing. A promise not given damns. But Luther knew the importance of the pronoun, the subject, is not a reference of the self to the self. Faith is not inner or subjective in that sense at all. Faith requires an external preacher—faith comes by hearing (Romans 10:17). But modernity has turned the "for me" of preaching into the "from me" of speculation—it has turned from God to the self as the source of the word.[70]

Luther refuses this move made in modernity and instead sticks with the "for me" of the Gospel. Disciples live as those who know that Christ Jesus is Savior, that is, He is gift, for them. In Luther's own words: "Christ is not the Law" (AE 26:137).

Luther does not use the word "atonement"[71] in either of the Catechisms. Instead, he speaks of how Christ Jesus made Himself "my Lord," by purchasing us not with gold or silver but with His precious blood, echoing 1 Peter 1:18–19. The willing victim who laid down His life won the victory not for Himself but for us "lost and condemned" creatures alienated from our Creator by sin and held captive to death and condemnation. Luther's language is not theoretical or abstract. Rather, his words paint the picture of a battle engaged in for us by the Son of God, who suffers in our place, fighting for us and winning our redemption not by a raw act of power but by submitting to the death of a sinner.

---

70 Steven Paulson, "Internal Clarity of Scripture and the Modern World: Luther and Erasmus Revisited," in *Hermeneutica Sacra: Studies in the Interpretation of Holy Scripture in the Sixteenth and Seventeenth Centuries*, ed. Torbjörn Johansson, Robert Kolb, and Johann Anselm Steiger (Berlin/New York: De Gruyter, 2010), 93.

71 Here see the essay by Kenneth Hagen, "Luther on Atonement—Reconfigured: Dedicated to the Memory of Dr. Robert Preus," in *The Word Does Everything: Key Concepts of Luther* (Milwaukee: Marquette University Press, 2016), 345–88.

The outcome of our Lord's reconciling work on the cross is that He now sets us under His lordship, "that I may be His own and live under Him in His kingdom and serve Him in everlasting righteousness, innocence, and blessedness, just as He is risen from the dead, lives and reigns to all eternity." Disciples are those people who are possessed by Christ; they belong to Him. They are under a new lordship. Transferred from the kingdom of darkness (see Colossians 1:13–14), they are no longer in servitude to the mastery of sin, terrified by condemnation, and destined to death.[72]

> **Disciples are those people who are possessed by Christ; they belong to Him.**

Luther uses three words to describe the life of the disciple: righteousness, innocence, and blessedness. Christ is our righteousness, that is, our justification before God. This righteousness is not based on the Law but on faith (see Galatians 2:20–21). Ian Siggins nicely captures the Reformer's thought:

> This, then, is the shape of righteousness: the grace and gift of forgiveness and newness of life, at that "mathematical point" where Christ our righteousness, through His Word and Spirit, dwells in us in His fullness by faith. Now, if Christ is our righteousness alone, He is also our holiness and sanctification by faith alone. Christ's righteousness is constantly defined in opposition to all so-called human righteousness; and in the same way, the only true holiness stands over and against every self-styled sanctity of man. Sanctification for Luther normally does not mean the process of moral

---

72    Also note Peters: "Luther permits the one who is making confession to be enwrapped completely by Christ who rules. From below and from time past, the one who was humiliated now holds onto the believer from above and from future time, the one who is elevated at the right hand of the Father holds that same believer. By means of His humiliation, which culminates in His death as an offering, Jesus Christ freed us from the tyranny of those powers of destruction: sin, death, and the devil. The event on the cross at Golgotha has seized the one who is making the confession and has transferred that believer into a new status through Holy Baptism; in our baptism, we were taken up into the event of Golgotha and were buried with Christ in His death as an offering. This redeeming activity of Christ, for me, opens at the same time an eschatological future, 'so that I might be His own and live under Him in His kingdom and serve Him in everlasting righteousness, innocence, and blessedness'" (*Creed*, 144).

purification or improvement in virtue, which is its chief connotation in post-Reformation theology. Rather, in the biblically strict sense, that is holy which is set apart for the worship and service of God.[73]

Just so, the disciple of Jesus Christ does not live in his or her only holiness but is set apart by the work and word of Christ to live under an alien righteousness, the righteous of another. That is, the disciple does not achieve righteousness by his or her own works, but it is received as a gift through faith in Christ.[74]

Under the righteousness of Christ, we live in innocence, for God does not hold our sins against us. Covered with the forgiveness of sins purchased and won by Christ, our consciences are cleansed from guilt. We have peace with God through faith in Christ. Our innocence does not mean that we never sin, but this sin is not held against us for the sake of Christ.

Under the lordship of the crucified and risen Christ, our existence is "blessedness."[75] We are on the receiving end of Christ's blessing. The words of the Beatitudes spoken to His first disciples are true of us who live under our Lord's words, declaring us to be heirs of His gracious kingdom. Blessedness means that we are no longer under the condemnation of the Law and the tyranny of sin and death. Instead, our lives are secure under the gracious reign of the Lord, whose resurrection from the dead declares His victory over these enemies. The stance of the disciple is not servile obedience to a demanding master but a life of blessedness in the new obedience of freedom that exists in Christ alone. Luther's robust confession of life in the kingdom of Christ Jesus is rooted in the apostolic proclamation that "if anyone is in Christ, he is a new creation. The old has passed away; behold, the new has

---

73    Siggins, 153–54.

74    Ernst Kinder rightly observes "Good works are the consequence of and not the prerequisite for justification," in *Evangelical: What Does It Really Mean?* Trans. Edward Schroeder and Marie Schroeder (St. Louis: Concordia Publishing House, 1968), 23. Disciples serve Christ because He has already made them His own.

75    Edmund Schlink says of this new existence: "To live under Christ in Christ's kingdom means to live with Christ; to serve him means to rule with him," in *Theology of the Lutheran Confessions,* 197.

come" (2 Corinthians 5:17) and "For freedom Christ has set us free" (Galatians 5:1).[76] This new life is guaranteed by Jesus Christ crucified for our sins and raised for our justification (see Romans 4:25). Once again, Luther's great hymn on justification echoes his treatment of the Second Article:

> Though he will shed My precious blood,
>> Me of My life bereaving,
> All this I suffer for your good;
>> Be steadfast and believing.
> Life will from death the vict'ry win;
> My innocence shall bear your sin,
>> And you are blest forever.
>
> (*LSB* 556:8)

# THE THIRD ARTICLE

Luther's exposition of the Third Article of the Creed demonstrates that this blessed life under the reign of Christ in His kingdom is not an existence brought about by our choice. Disciples do not make the kingdom or acquire it for themselves; they are brought into Christ's kingdom by the Holy Spirit as He calls sinners by the Gospel to live by faith in the reconciling work of Christ. Christ and the Holy Spirit go together. Where Christ is, there is His Spirit.[77] It is only by the Holy Spirit that we are brought to confess "Jesus is Lord" (1 Corinthians 12:3). There is no faith without the Holy Spirit, and this faith is trust in Christ as He gives Himself to us in the Gospel. The content and object of this faith is none other than Christ, crucified and raised from the

---

76    Hans Joachim Iwand gives an apt description of this freedom: "That is precisely the heavenly gift that Luther finds in the New Righteousness; the freedom of the children of God who do work simply that it may be done, but who do not need to any work at all in order to know that they live by God's grace," in *The Righteousness of Faith According to Luther,* trans. Randi H. Lundell (Eugene: Wipf and Stock, 2008), 67.

77    Sasse observes, "The New Testament's view of the Holy Spirit can be stated in one sentence: Where Christ is, there is the Holy Spirit; where the Holy Spirit is, there is Christ. Christ and the Holy Spirit belong together. Faith can have no experience of the reality of the Holy Spirit unless it is somehow an experience of the true and living presence of Christ. There can be no faith in that present Christ, no confession that Jesus is Lord, unless it is mediated through the Holy Spirit," in "Jesus Christ Is Lord," 31.

dead. Oswald Bayer helpfully reminds us that this faith is not a generic trust in something unknown and unnamed: "Faith is in fact completely an act of trust, but it is trust that is grounded and connected. If I do not know the one in whom I place my trust and what I entrust to him, then the faith relationship—no matter how sincerely and earnestly it may be—remains empty and aimless."[78] The Spirit-wrought faith that saves is faith in Christ alone.

> **There is no faith without the Holy Spirit, and this faith is trust in Christ as He gives Himself to us in the Gospel.**

It is the work of the Spirit to make holy. "But God's Spirit alone is called a Holy Spirit, that is, the one who has made us holy and still makes us holy" (LC II 36; K-W, 435). The hallowing work of the Spirit is carried out through the Gospel, and it is directed toward the resurrection of the body and life everlasting. The Spirit carries the verbs. He calls, gathers, enlightens, and sanctifies. In doing this work, He keeps the whole Christian Church on earth with Jesus Christ in the true faith.

The Spirit delivers to us what the Son of God obtained. Jesus established His kingdom by His death and resurrection. Sanctification is not our project but the Spirit's work as He brings us into Christ's holy kingdom. Luther describes it like this:

> **Just as the Son obtains dominion by purchasing us through his birth, death, and resurrection, etc., so the Holy Spirit effects our being made holy through the following: the community of saints or Christian church, the forgiveness of sins, the resurrection of the body, and the life everlasting. That is, he first leads us into his holy community, placing us in the church's lap, where he preaches to us and brings us to Christ.**
>
> (LC II 37; K-W, 435–36).

---

78 Oswald Bayer, *Martin Luther's Theology: A Contemporary Interpretation*, trans. Thomas H. Trapp (Grand Rapids: Eerdmans, 2008), 240.

The Spirit is at work in the word of the cross, not merely informing us about Jesus but declaring that He is your Lord, for He has died to redeem you and now lives to give you His life. Through this message the Spirit enlightens darkened minds with His gifts: the forgiveness of sins, peace with God, and the promise of the resurrection of our bodies to life in God's eternal kingdom. The Spirit communicates this through His Word. He does more than just inform. His Word actually bestows what it promises.

While the Spirit convicts the world of sin through the Law (see John 16:8), His proper work is to promote the promises of Christ Jesus. Luther captures this in his sermons on John:

> Christ says: "He will bear witness of none but Me. This will be known as the Holy Spirit's sermon. Therefore He will not be a Moses or a preacher of the Law such as you have had and still have; but I will put into His mouth another and more sublime sermon than the one Moses gave to you. Moses taught you nothing but the Law or the Ten Commandments, which he had received from God; he told you what to do and what not to do. But this One will make of you preachers and confessors who tell and testify, not of their own deeds and life but of Me."
>
> (AE 24:295)

Moses would be the voice of divine condemnation. The Spirit is the Comforter, who preaches the consolation of the forgiveness of sins on account of Christ's blood. Through this Gospel alone, He calls sinners to be His own, creating disciples who live as His Holy Church.

There is no discipleship apart from the Spirit's words. To follow Jesus is to be on the receiving end of His words that "are spirit and life" (John 6:63). Created by the Word of God, the Holy Christian Church is the place of disciples. Disciples are not freelance followers of Jesus, each living according to his or her own instincts and insights. Called by the Gospel, disciples are gathered in Christ's Church, His "holy community" as the Large Catechism calls it. "In this Christian church He daily and richly forgives all my sins and the sins of all

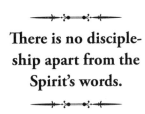

**There is no disciple-ship apart from the Spirit's words.**

believers." Where the forgiveness of sins purchased and won by Christ is preached and bestowed, there is the church. The church is neither an institution of salvation nor a collective of like-minded seekers after God, but it is that holy community of believers in Jesus Christ who are created, sustained, and preserved by the Gospel.

Just as God the Father "richly and daily provides me with all that I need to support this body and life" in the First Article, so in the Third Article, the Holy Spirit now "daily and richly forgives all my sins and the sins of all believers." God's design for the bestowal of the forgiveness of sins is abundant and generous, reflected in the multiple means or instruments He has instituted. Luther unpacks this in the Large Catechism:

> Further we believe that in this Christian community we have the forgiveness of sins, which takes place through the holy sacraments and absolution as well as through all the comforting words of the entire gospel. This encompasses everything that is to be preached about the sacraments and, in short, the entire gospel and all the official responsibilities of the Christian community. Forgiveness is constantly needed, for although God's grace has been acquired by Christ, and holiness has been wrought by the Holy Spirit through God's Word in the unity of the Christian church, yet we are never without sin because we carry our flesh around our neck.

> (LC II 54; K-W, 438)

Luther is making the point that the sanctifying work of the Holy Spirit is not past tense. The confession "I cannot by my own reason or strength believe in Jesus Christ, my Lord, or come to Him" is not a statement that is limited to the moment of conversion. I could not now believe that Jesus is my Lord without the Spirit working daily to forgive my sins and keep me with Jesus Christ in the one true faith. Just as I could not by my own resources of reason, determination of the will, or moral effort make myself a disciple of Jesus, neither can I keep myself in faith. The Spirit keeps me in saving faith through His appointed means. Luther continues,

> Therefore everything in this Christian community is so ordered that everyone may daily obtain full forgiveness of sins through the Word and signs appointed to comfort and encourage our consciences as long as we live on earth. Although we have sin, the Holy Spirit sees to it that it does not harm us because we are a part of this Christian community. Here there is full forgiveness of sins, both in that God forgives us and that we forgive, bear with, and aid one another.
>
> (LC II 55; K-W, 438)[79]

The Church created by the Holy Spirit is not a holy club of spiritually superior individuals but is broken sinners gathered and sustained by the Gospel of the forgiveness of sins in Christ alone. Where this forgiveness is preached and delivered in Word and Sacrament, the Spirit creates faith in the hearts of those who hear the Gospel. The reference

**Where this forgiveness is preached and delivered in Word and Sacrament, the Spirit creates faith in the hearts of those who hear the Gospel.**

---

79    Here also the Smalcald Articles, where Luther states that through the Gospel God gives us help against sin in multiple means of preaching, Baptism, Lord's Supper, absolution, and the mutual consolation of fellow disciples "because God is extravagantly rich in his grace" (SA III 4; K-W, 319).

point for the Church is always this Gospel. The Church is a creature of God's Word, and within this community the Word is proclaimed for the forgiveness of sins.

The forgiveness of sins is not simply the initial activity of the Holy Spirit as though our justification before God was a beginning stage that we now move beyond to a higher level called discipleship. No, disciples live in the community of God's Church by the forgiveness of sins. We cannot live without the forgiveness of sin. The life of the disciple is constituted in the forgiveness of sins for the sake of Christ. The forgiveness of sins is no mere psychological device for living with one's sense of guilt and shame; it is the reality of God's righteousness for us in Christ. As such, it is the air that the disciple breathes.[80]

In the forgiveness of sins, there is the promise of the resurrection. Christ's absolution anticipates the verdict of the Last Day, so the Third Article of the Creed draws us toward the fact that the Spirit "will raise me and all the dead, and give eternal life to me and all believers in Christ." The Spirit's work of "daily and richly" forgiving my sins and the sins of all believers will come to culmination on what Luther often referred to as "the dear Last Day," where the disciple is once and for all finished with sin, death, and the devil.

> Meanwhile, because holiness has begun and is growing daily, we await the time when our flesh will be put to death, will be buried with all its uncleanness, and will come forth gloriously and arise to complete and perfect holiness in a new, eternal life. Now, however, we remain only halfway pure and holy. The Holy Spirit must always work in us through the Word, granting us daily forgiveness until we attain to that life where

---

80    Oswald Bayer says it well: "Forgiveness of sins is not what it meant to Schleiermacher—an enlightenment and empowerment of one's own consciousness of God. It is a reality that goes far beyond one's consciousness, it describes how all the powers of destruction that are at enmity with God and humanity are overpowered," in *Martin Luther's Theology*, 222.

> there will be no more forgiveness. In that life there will be only perfectly pure and holy people, full of integrity and righteousness, completely freed from sin, death, and all misfortune, living in new, immortal, and glorified bodies.

(LC II 57–58; K-W, 438)

All human beings will be raised from the dead, but only believers in Christ will receive the gift of eternal life. The Last Day brings with it a dual outcome: final condemnation of the secure sinner or joyful acquittal of the broken sinner. The universal character of God's grace in Christ does not lead Luther to the heresy of universalism.[81] Hell is the eternal consequence of unbelief. Everlasting life with Christ is the outcome of Spirit-worked faith.

Living under the verdict of the Spirit's Word, which declares us righteous for the sake of the death and resurrection of Christ, the disciple lives in patience and hope toward the final victory. "Now we wait in faith for this to be accomplished through the Word" (LC II 62; K-W, 439). It is in this certain confidence that disciples of Jesus Christ live and die. By the Spirit's Word, we were brought to faith in Christ, sustained in that faith throughout the days of our earthly pilgrimage, and at the end it will be by that same Word that we will be raised from the dead to follow the Lamb forever.

Luther's hearty "This is most certainly true" at the end of his explanation of each article of the Creed can be understood only with reference to the surety of the triune God's work. Certainty is not a reference to the credibility of the disciple but the fidelity of God to His promises. Because God carries the verbs, disciples are given certainty, that is, confidence in God, the Father, Son,

---

81    Here see Jeffrey Silcock: "Luther preserves the biblical contrast between the universal resurrection and the bestowal of life to believers only. He follows the dogmatic tradition of the church in distinguishing between the universal resurrection of all people and the particularity of eternal life only to those who have faith in Christ. He holds to the eternal damnation of unbelievers but does not say much about it as his focus is on redemption. Luther nowhere countenances Origen's theory of *apokatastasis* (universal restoration), which teaches that all will be saved, including the devil," in "A Lutheran Approach to Eschatology" *Lutheran Quarterly* 31:4 (Winter 207): 382. For more on this issue, see *Confessing the Gospel: A Lutheran Approach to Systematic Theology,* 2:1154–69.

and Holy Spirit. This is God-certainty, for it is predicated not on the human ego but in the fidelity of God, who wills, accomplishes, and delivers our redemption.[82] Therefore we may agree with Ernst Käsemann that "genuine discipleship is a miracle of the Holy Spirit."[83]

---

82    Also see Helmut Thielicke: "False security is what results when my nature takes measures to help itself; it leaves me still in the sphere of my inner ego," in *Theological Ethics*, 1:313. On the other hand, certainty is anchored in the work of the Trinity.

83    Ernst Käsemann, *On Being a Disciple of the Crucified Nazarene*, trans. Roy Harrisville (Grand Rapids: Eerdmans, 2010), 315.

## FOR FURTHER REFLECTION AND STUDY: CONNECTIONS WITH LUTHER'S SMALL CATECHISM WITH EXPLANATION 2017

1. How is the Creed different from the Ten Commandments? (See p. 128.)

2. What does the Creed teach us about God on the basis of the Holy Scriptures? (See pp. 130–32.)

3. When we acknowledge that we are creatures, what are we saying about God? (See pp. 133–38.)

4. How does the biblical account of creation differ from other explanations? (See pp. 138–39.)

5. What does it mean to be made in the image of God? (See pp. 139–41.)

6. How does God demonstrate His goodness and kindness in creating us? (See pp. 146–49.)

7. How does the First Article equip us to address the question of evil in the world? (See pp. 150–54.)

8. What is the relationship between God's original creation (Genesis 1–2) and God's ongoing work of creation? (See pp. 156–58.)

9. How are creation and redemption bound together? (See pp. 158–59.)

10. What is our response to the gift of creation? (See pp. 159–63.)

11. What are we saying when we call Jesus "Lord"? (See pp. 164–66.)

12. How is it that Jesus is both true God and true man? (See pp. 167–75.)

13. What does it mean to "redeem"? (See pp. 177–81.)

14. Why is the resurrection of Jesus essential to the Christian faith? (See pp. 181–83.)

15. What is meant by the states of "humiliation" and "exaltation"? (See pp. 183–87.)

16. What does it mean to be the possession of Christ and live under Him in His kingdom? (See pp. 189–92.)

17. How is the Third Article connected to the Second Article? (See pp. 195–97.)

18. What is faith? (See pp. 196–97.)

19. What does the Holy Spirit do through the Gospel? (See pp. 197–98.)

20. Who sanctifies us? What is the relationship of good works to sanctification? (See pp. 198–200.)

21. How does the Holy Spirit keep us in faith? (See p. 200.)

22. Where does the Holy Spirit do His work? (See pp. 205–8.)

23. What is the outcome of the Holy Spirit's work? (See pp. 222–29.)

*Chapter 4*

———✦·⊹—●⊹·✦———

# The LORD's Prayer:
# Jesus Teaches His Disciples to Pray

**It is a mark of His kingdom that it contains poor, crying, praying people who suffer much on His account. Likewise His way and rule is none other than to help, hear, and lend assistance to the poor, the afflicted, the dying, and the sinners.**

MARTIN LUTHER ON PSALM 102:17
(AE 14:184)

Disciples have no sufficiency in and of themselves. Indeed, they are "poor, crying, praying people" whose lives are lived under the cross, buffeted by disappointment and suffering. But it is to such people that Jesus gives words to come before His Father, the God of all mercy and consolation. The Lord's Prayer is both a diagnosis of our neediness in this fallen creation and an account of the abundance of God's fatherly provisions for His children. Luther recognized that prayer is not a manipulation of God but the cry of faith.[84] The Lord's Prayer is, in the words of Friedrich Mildenberger, "a catalogue of human needs drawn up by God so that we would know what to ask God for any time we need help."[85]

---

84   For a very helpful overview of Luther's teaching and practice of prayer, see Mary Jane Haemig, "Prayer," in *The Oxford Encyclopedia of Martin Luther*, vol. 3, ed. Derek R. Nelson and Paul R. Hinlicky (New York: Oxford University Press, 2017), 156–70.

85   Friedrich Mildenberger, *Theology of the Lutheran Confessions*, 148.

Jesus teaches His disciples to pray (Matthew 6:5–15; Luke 11:1–13), not with the repetitious babbling of an uncertain heart but with the sure confidence that is firmly anchored in the Father's command and promise. A decade or so before he prepared the Small Catechism, the Reformer addressed false understandings of prayer in two tracts. In *On Rogationtide Prayer and Procession*, written in 1519 to provide an evangelical corrective to the abuses that had accumulated around the blessing of the fields associated with *Rogate* Sunday (the Fifth Sunday of Easter), Luther anchors the practice of prayer in the sure and certain promises of God:

> **First, we must have a promise or a pledge from God. We must reflect on this promise and remind God of it, and in that way be emboldened to pray with confidence. If God had not enjoined us to pray and if he had not promised fulfillment, no creature would be able to obtain so much as a kernel of grain despite all his petitions.**
>
> (AE 42:87)

God's promises alone give disciples the certainty that their prayers are heard by the Father and are pleasing to Him.

In a second piece on prayer from 1519, *An Exposition of the Lord's Prayer for Simple Laymen*, Luther sees the praying of the Lord's Prayer as an exercise of faith taking God at His Word, for it is "from these words of Christ we learn about both the words and the manner, that is, they tell us how and for what we are to pray" (AE 42:19). Here Luther also makes the point that the Lord's Prayer is the source of all genuine prayer: "Since our Lord is the author of this prayer, it is without a doubt the most sublime, the loftiest, and the most excellent. If he, the good and faithful Teacher, had known a better one, he would surely have taught us that too" (AE 42:21). Both of these early treatments of the Lord's Prayer contain key themes in Luther's understanding of prayer that will be developed and sharpened in the Catechisms.

Already in 1519, in *An Exposition of the Lord's Prayer*, Luther reflects a parent-child intimacy, later expanded in the Small Catechism, when he writes that with this prayer "the heart says more than the lips" (AE 42:23). Ten years later, now a father himself, he spells it out in his explanation of the Introduction of the Lord's Prayer in the Small Catechism:

> **With these words God tenderly invites us to believe that He is our true Father and that we are His true children, so that with all boldness and confidence we may ask Him as dear children ask their dear Father.**[86]

Faith clings to the words of the Father and so comes before Him, not in the duplicity of doubt or the cowardice of unbelief but in the confidence that the Father Almighty, Maker of heaven and earth, is, in fact, the God and Father of our Lord Jesus Christ. Discipleship is dialogical, that is, those who know God are speaking back to Him in the words He has given us.[87] Disciples recognize that they have access to God by way of His promises in Christ Jesus and can deal with Him only through faith.[88]

Disciples address God as "our Father." The language of fatherhood is not that of metaphor or analogy.[89] While God does possess characteristics we often associate with human fathers—strength, kindness, compassion, and so forth—the prayer that teaches us

---

86    Birgit Stolt has shown that after Luther himself became a father, his delight in calling God "Father" intensified. See Birgit Stolt, "Martin Luther on God as Father," *Lutheran Quarterly* 8 (1994): 385–95. In these writings, she notes that "Luther feels he is talking with this kind of father in his prayers: a father not principally awe-inspiring but a source of trust and joy" (392).

87    Werner Elert observes, "Man prays because he believes in God's promises, not (to use Ritschl's formulation) in God's government in the universe. He prays, therefore, with confidence. Otherwise it would not be a prayer in faith. His confidence springs from the fact that God himself opens the dialogue, and consists in the assurance that God himself will have the last word and will not terminate the communication prematurely. My response does not go out into a vacuum but will be heard by him and heard according to his promise," in *The Christian Ethos*, 308–9.

88    Here see Luther in *The Babylonian Captivity of the Church* (1520): "For God does not deal, nor has he ever dealt, with man otherwise than through a word of promise, as I have said. We in turn cannot deal with God otherwise than through faith in the Word of his promise" (AE 36:42).

89    We are not free to call God by another name, such as "Parent" or "Mother," as feminist theologians have suggested in recent decades. God is the Father who is made known by His Son. To forsake the name of Father is finally to resort to what Luther calls "the hidden God." Only in Christ do we find God the Father. For more on this point, see Gerhard Forde, "Naming the One Who Is Above Us," in *Speaking the Christian God: The Holy Trinity and the Challenge of Feminism,* ed. Alvin F. Kimbel Jr. (Grand Rapids: Eerdmans, 1992), 110–19.

addresses God as Father.[90] He is not merely *like* a father, but He *is* our Father, for this God has a Son. Baptized into Christ Jesus, we now are all His sons (both male and female) through faith (Galatians 3:26–29). All who are sons of God through faith are disciples, learning how to call Jesus' Father "our Father," just as we pray in the ancient Pentecost hymn:

> Come, holy Light, guide divine,
> Now cause the Word of life to shine.
>     Teach us to know our God aright
>     And call Him Father with delight.
> From ev'ry error keep us free;
>     Let none but Christ our master be
>     That we in living faith abide,
> In Him, our Lord, with all our might confide.
>         Alleluia, alleluia!

(LSB 497:2; © 1941 CPH)

# THE INTRODUCTION

Just as the First Commandment interlocks with the First Article of the Creed, even so the words "Our Father who art in heaven" draw disciples back to the First Commandment. The God who is feared, loved, and trusted above all things is no nameless deity, no anonymous architect of the universe or impersonal ground of being, but the Father. Luther said, "He who does not call on God or pray to Him in trouble certainly does not consider Him as God" (AE 14:61). Thus, for the disciple, prayer is "a practical way of performing the First Commandment."[91] When disciples open their mouths to pray the Lord's Prayer, they are recognizing that they have a God who is trustworthy in this perilous journey

---

90    Here note Joachim Jeremias: "He [Jesus] gives them a share in his sonship and empowers them as his disciples, to speak with their heavenly Father in just such a familiar, trusting way as a child would speak with his father," in *The Lord's Prayer*, trans. John Reumann (Philadelphia: Fortress Press, 1964), 20.

91    Dennis Ngien, *Luther's Theology of the Cross: Christ in Luther's Sermons on John* (Eugene, OR: Cascade Books, 2018), 155.

through life in a fallen world. Luther captured this thought already in his 1519 treatise *An Exposition of the Lord's Prayer for Simple Laymen*, where he wrote that the Introduction "says, as it were, 'O Father, you are in heaven, while I, your poor child, am in misery on earth, far away from you surrounded, by many perils, in need and want, among the devils, the greatest enemies, and in much danger'" (AE 42:23).

Discipleship is not a futile attempt to trace the steps of an unknown God, hidden in awe and majesty, but is walking by faith, trusting in the promises of the God who has made Himself known to us in Jesus as our Father in heaven. "Take Bethlehem and Golgotha out of the world and the cry of God will be silenced," wrote Helmut Thielicke, "and praying becomes meaningless."[92] Without God's revelation of His fatherly heart in Christ Jesus, prayer would be futile exercise, an act of unfulfilled desperation in attempting to reach an

> **Discipleship is not a futile attempt to trace the steps of an unknown God, hidden in awe and majesty, but is walking by faith.**

unreachable God. But the living God has spoken to us in His Son, showing us His heart, which pulsates with favor toward His frail and fragile creatures. In merciful condescension, He comes to us not in wrath but in grace. He does not keep His distance from sinners but tenderly invites us to call upon Him as dear children speak to a dear father. Father is not a title that we hang on God but is the very name He has given us to call upon Him in trouble and pray to Him for every need. In a sermon preached in the World War II era, Walter Lüthi said, "The Devil loves anonymity, but God has a name."[93] God's name is Father. It is hallowed because it belongs to Him, and it proclaims to us who He is.

---

92 Helmut Thielicke, *Our Heavenly Father: Sermons on the Lord's Prayer,* trans. John W. Doberstein (New York: Harper and Row, 1960), 32.

93 Walter Lüthi, *The Lord's Prayer: An Exposition,* trans. Kurt Schoenenberger (Edinburgh: Oliver and Boyd, 1962), 10.

# THE FIRST PETITION

The Father's name taken up on lips of the disciple is holy. The Catechism reminds us that the holiness of God's name is self-contained; it is holy in and of itself. The focus of the praying of this petition is that God's name may be kept holy among His disciples by what we say and do. Peters nicely captures Luther's intention: "As we Christians call upon Him in the Lord's Prayer as our Father and confess ourselves as His own in the Creed, we stand up for His honor in doctrine and life, in word and deed among mankind."[94]

Both doctrine and life come under the canopy of the First Petition. Doctrine enjoys a particular priority, for Luther understands doctrine as the teaching that comes from God. Because it is of God, true doctrine contains nothing that is defective or incomplete. Life, on the other hand, is always lacking among disciples because the old Adam stubbornly clings to those who belong to the Father.[95] When we pray "Hallowed be Thy name," we are confessing our own lack of holiness, even as we take shelter in the holy name into which we are baptized.

> **The old Adam stubbornly clings to those who belong to the Father.**

To pray this petition is to confess our own neediness, for we have not kept our Lord's name holy, as the Second Commandment demonstrates. This point is made with clarity in Luther's exposition of the petition in the Large Catechism:

---

94   Albrecht Peters, *Commentary on Luther's Catechisms: Lord's Prayer*, trans. Daniel Thies (St. Louis: Concordia Publishing House, 2011), 63.

95   Here note Luther in his 1535 lectures on Galatians: "Therefore, as I often warn you, doctrine must be carefully distinguished from life. Doctrine is heaven; life is earth. In life there is sin, error, uncleanness, and misery, mixed, as the saying goes, 'with vinegar.' Here love should condone, tolerate, be deceived, trust, hope, and endure all things (1 Cor. 13:7); here the forgiveness of sins should have complete sway, provided that sin and error are not defended. But just as there is no error in doctrine, so there is no need for any forgiveness of sins. Therefore there is no comparison at all between doctrine and life. 'One dot' of doctrine is worth more than 'heaven and earth' (Matt. 5:18); therefore we do not permit the slightest offense against it. But we can be lenient toward errors of life. For we, too, err daily in our life and conduct; so do all the saints, as they earnestly confess in the Lord's Prayer and the Creed. But by the grace of God our doctrine is pure; we have all the articles of faith solidly established in Sacred Scripture. The devil would dearly love to corrupt and overthrow these; that is why he attacks us so cleverly with this specious argument about not offending against love and harmony among the churches" (AE 27:41–42).

So you see that in this petition we pray for exactly the same thing that God demands in the Second Commandment: that his name should not be taken in vain by swearing, cursing, deceiving etc., but used rightly to the praise and glory of God. Whoever uses God's name for any sort of wrong profanes and desecrates this holy name, as in the past a church was said to be desecrated when a murder or other crime had been committed in it, or when a monstrance or relic was profaned, thus rendering unholy by misuse that which is holy in itself. This petition, then, is simple and clear if we only understand the language, namely, that to "hallow" means the same as our idiom "to praise, extol, and honor" both in word and deed.

(LC III 45–46; K-W, 446)

Because it is His name, it is holy—set apart by God Himself—for the express purpose that we might know Him and use His name as He intends His disciples to use it.

Disciples are not praying for the hallowing of their own names but that God's name—Father, Son, and Holy Spirit, inscribed on them in Holy Baptism—might be honored and glorified with their lips, which confess His truth and lives that are consecrated to the priestly service of the neighbor in their neediness. This is the spiritual worship of which Paul speaks in Romans 12:1–2, and it is carried out in the world where disciples live as salt and light (see Matthew 5:13–16). God's name is hallowed within the callings where the disciples live in this world.

# THE SECOND PETITION

When we hallow God's name by calling upon Him in faith, we are also praying for the coming of His kingdom. The First Petition is bound up with the Second Petition, where Jesus teaches

His disciples to pray for the coming of the Father's kingdom. When the Scriptures speak of the kingdom of God (or the kingdom of heaven), they are not referring to a domain that is political or geographical or to a commonwealth constructed by the will and efforts of human beings. God's kingdom is the reign that He establishes, sustains, and brings to consummation. To paraphrase Luther, disciples do not prepare the kingdom but the kingdom is prepared for disciples.[96]

Disciples do not build God's kingdom; that task belongs to the King alone. It is the good pleasure of the Father to give His disciples His kingdom (see Luke 12:32). It is a kingdom prepared for us from the foundation of the world (see Matthew 25:34).[97]

Luther reminds us, "The kingdom of God certainly comes by itself without our prayer, but we pray in this petition that it may come to us also." We are recipients of the kingdom where Jesus Christ is ruling over sinners with the word of reconciliation, forgiving sins and giving newness of life to all who trust in Him. God's kingdom is not an evolutionary development, coming in incremental stages only to reach fulfillment in an earthly golden age presided over by the triumphant Christ. Rather, Christ's kingdom comes now in time as the crucified Lord gathers a people for Himself through the preaching of the Gospel. Luther gives this succinct definition of God's kingdom in the Large Catechism. The kingdom is

> **Christ's kingdom comes now in time as the crucified Lord gathers a people for Himself through the preaching of the Gospel.**

what we heard above in the Creed, namely, that God sent his Son, Christ our LORD, into the world to redeem and deliver us from the power of the devil, to bring

---

96    Here see Werner Elert: "Luther says in reply to Erasmus: 'The kingdom is not being prepared; it has been prepared. In fact, the sons of the kingdom are being prepared; they are not preparing the kingdom,'" in *The Structure of Lutheranism*, 494. The full Luther citation is found in AE 33:153.

97    The thought of these passages is beautifully captured in Heinz Werner Zimmermann's hymn "Have No Fear, Little Flock" (*LSB* 735) as stanza 1 proclaims, "For the Father has chosen To give you the Kingdom" (© 1973 CPH).

**us to himself, and to rule us as a king of righteousness, life, and salvation against sin, death, and an evil conscience. To this end he also gave his Holy Spirit to deliver this to us through his holy Word and to enlighten and strengthen us in faith by his power.**

(LC III 51; K-W, 446)

In this portion of the Large Catechism, Luther is echoing the words of Paul in Colossians 1:13–14, "He [Christ] has delivered us from the domain of darkness and transferred us to the kingdom of His beloved Son, in whom we have redemption, the forgiveness of sins." The kingdom is the gift of the Father established in His Son and extended to us by the Spirit in the proclamation of the Gospel.

The kingdom of God is not an empire visible to the eye. It is a kingdom accessed by the ear. The gift of God's kingdom comes in tandem with the gift of the Holy Spirit, who brings us to faith and keeps us there. Here we may note that Luther is demonstrating a parallelism between the First and Second Petitions as "God's name is kept holy when the Word of God is taught in its truth and purity, and we, as the children of God, also lead holy lives according to it" is echoed in God giving us His Spirit so that "we believe His holy Word and lead godly lives here in time and there in eternity." Once again, we see that the pattern of discipleship is faith and love, doctrine and life. These are distinguished but never pulled apart. Inwardly, we live in Christ's kingdom by faith as outwardly we live a life of love toward the neighbor within the worldly realm. In the words of Gustaf Wingren, "Faith is entrance into heaven. Love is rightly at home on earth."[98]

Disciples live as free citizens of the kingdom of heaven now by faith, even as they wait in eager expectation for its final consummation with the return of the Lord to judge the living and the dead. Discipleship always has before it the eschatological

---

98    Gustaf Wingren, *Luther on Vocation,* , 21.

horizon, the certain and sure hope that one's trust in the Lord's promises will finally be vindicated when faith gives way to sight. So we are bold to continually pray, "Thy kingdom come." This prayer is prayed in the confidence of hope that is not limited by human categories of pessimism or optimism but in the certainty of God's promise.[99]

# THE THIRD PETITION

The First and Second Petitions are fused together in the Third Petition, where disciples pray, "Thy will be done." Disciples confess God's name and live in His kingdom. This means that they will be under attack. Therefore, Luther begins his exposition of the Third Petition in the Large Catechism with the observation that by embracing the first two petitions, Christians are emboldened to implore God for His help, for alone we can hold fast to neither His name or kingdom:

> These two points embrace all that pertains to God's glory and to our salvation, in which we appropriate God with all his treasures. But there is just as great need for us to keep firm hold on these two things and never to allow ourselves to be torn from them. In a good government there is need not only for good builders and rulers, but for defenders, protectors, and vigilant guardians. So here also; although we have prayed for what is most necessary—for the gospel, for faith, and for the Holy Spirit, that he may govern us who have been redeemed from the power of the devil—we must also pray that God will cause his will to be done. If we try to hold these treasures fast, we will have to suffer an astonishing number of attacks

---

99   Here see Bayer: "Luther's distinctive courage, which goes beyond optimism and pessimism, is grounded in Baptism," in *Living by Faith: Justification and Sanctification*, trans. Geoffrey W. Bromiley (Grand Rapids: Eerdmans, 2003), 66.

and assaults from all who venture to hinder and thwart
the fulfillment of the first two petitions.

(LC III 60–61; K-W, 448)

Thus the first two petitions for the heavenly treasures of God's
name and kingdom necessitate that disciples pray for God's will
to be done.

Disciples are not left to guess what
God's will is for their lives. We come to
know the good and gracious will of our
Father only in Christ Jesus. His will is to
strengthen and keep "us firm in His Word
and faith until we die." This, the Catechism
asserts, is "His good and gracious will."

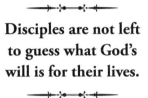

**Disciples are not left
to guess what God's
will is for their lives.**

There is a dual action involved with God accomplishing His
will among us. The Catechism speaks of what Luther elsewhere
refers to as God's alien work. This is God's work of opposition to
all that would stand in the way of our salvation. Here God actively
does battle against that triad of enemies: "the devil, the world,
and our sinful nature." Because these three are God's enemies,
they are our enemies as well. God makes no peace treaty with
them, and neither may His disciples.

God's alien work is not accomplished without suffering.[100] He
is, after all, breaking and hindering "every evil plan and purpose
of the devil, the world, and our sinful nature." What Luther
calls God's proper work, that is, the work that reflects His very
nature, is our everlasting salvation. He graciously wills in Christ
to bring us to saving faith and keep us in that faith until we come
to eternal life. The Formula of Concord speaks of the great clarity
and consolation that this teaching gives disciples:

---

100    This distinction between the alien and proper work of God is beautifully illustrated by Helmut Thielicke: "God
drives us with scourges out of the temple of our self-worship and smashes the Babylonian tower of our pride before
he becomes our Father. God plunges us into a sea of uncertainty about ourselves and our aimless unrest, before he
gives us peace," in *Between God and Satan,* trans. C. C. Barber (Grand Rapids: Eerdmans, 1958), 9.

This doctrine also gives us wonderful comfort in crosses and trials, that in his counsel before time began God determined and decreed that he would stand by us in every trouble, grant us patience, give us comfort, create hope, and provide a way out of all things so that we may be saved [cf. 1 Cor. 10:13]. Likewise, Paul treats this matter in such a comforting way in Romans 8[:28–39], pointing out that in his intention before time began God preordained what sort of crosses and sufferings he would use to conform each one of his elect to "the image of his Son," and that the cross of each should and must "work together for the good" of that person, because they are "called according to his purpose." On this basis Paul concluded with certainty and without doubt that neither "hardship nor distress . . . neither death nor life . . . will be able to separate us from the love of God in Christ Jesus, our Lord."

(FC SD XI 48–49; K-W, 648–49)[101]

The petition "Thy will be done" embraces both God's alien and proper work. The disciple is enabled to pray this petition with the confidence of the apostle Paul in Philippians 1: "And I am sure of this, that He who began a good work in you will bring it to completion at the day of Jesus Christ" (v. 6). Disciples learn how to pray the Third Petition not as a cry of resignation to an unalterable fate for simply as submission to a power stronger than themselves, but as a joyful confession that because of Christ Jesus, God's will for us is eternally good.

The Third Petition, like the whole of the Lord's Prayer, is prayed under the sign of the cross. It is prayed with this recognition:

---

101    For a biblically informed and pastorally responsible treatment of the biblical teaching of God's will in the doctrine of election, see Robert Kolb, "Election," in *Confessing the Gospel: A Lutheran Approach to Systematic Theology*, vol. 2, ed. Samuel Nafzger et al. (St. Louis: Concordia Publishing House, 2017), 1195–1261.

Our life is that of cross and resurrection—none can escape the pain that life brings, especially as we seek to do what is right in the world. Yet such painful events are not beyond God's work. God works through the crushing events of life precisely to raise the dead, to call sinners as his own, to remove them as the centers of their own universes and replace them with himself at the center. God provides us a new path upon which to walk, good works which serve our neighbor, and a grateful heart from which to praise him.[102]

Disciples pray "Thy will be done" in the midst of a collapsing creation that is sustained only by the Word and promise of the triune God. So Luther looks, Peters observes,

at the dangerous and thorn-filled way that the Word of God and with it all Christendom and every individual believer still has in front of them before the world encompassing goal is reached. That winding way veiled from us, Luther moves into the bright light of the fatherly, gracious will of God, which is revealed to us through Christ in the Holy Spirit.[103]

It is only in Christ that we can pray "Thy will be done," not as fatalists but as children who walk not by sight but by faith in a sure and certain promise.

## THE FOURTH PETITION

Jesus' prayer has disciples giving priority to the things of God: His name, kingdom, and will. Only with the Fourth Petition are we given to pray for those things that impact our temporal life.

---

102    Mark C. Mattes, "The Theology of the Cross Speaks Today," in *Comfortable Words: Essays in Honor of Paul F. M. Zahl*, ed. John D. Koch Jr. and Todd H. W. Brewer (Eugene: Pickwick Publications, 2013), 165.

103    Peters, *The Lord's Prayer*, 115.

The Fourth Petition draws us back to the First Article. It is true that disciples live not by bread alone but by the bread of God's Word, but disciples still must eat! The fact that we have Christ, the bread of life, does not negate our need for daily bread, the ordinary stuff needed for creaturely life to be sustained and to flourish. The gift of daily bread enables the physical existence of disciples: "The group of disciples prays for a common sustenance of all life and therein for the basis for subsistence and the space to live for the proclamation of the coming kingdom."[104]

Daily bread (or the perceived lack thereof) is the cause for worry and anxiety generated by unbelief, which Jesus forbids in Matthew 6:25–34. Where God is not trusted to provide these elementary needs that sustain human life, there can only be a paralyzing fear of deprivation and loss of life.

In the place of anxiety over the things needed to sustain this body and life, disciples are given the Fourth Petition. The Lord of heaven and earth provides for all human beings whether or not they trust in Him, for He is the God who provides for His creatures "only out of fatherly, divine goodness and mercy, without any merit in me." Luther echoes the words of Jesus, "For [God] makes His sun rise on the evil and on the good, and sends rain on the just and on the unjust" (Matthew 5:45), when he explains that "God certainly gives daily bread to everyone without our prayers, even to all evil people."

God gives disciples their daily bread, not because they ask for it but because it is His fatherly nature to be the benefactor of His creatures. Asking for daily bread is rather a recognition of our dependence on His goodness. Recognition gives birth to thanksgiving. "We pray in this petition," says Luther, "that God would lead us to realize this and to receive our daily bread with thanksgiving."

Thanksgiving is more than an interior sense of gratitude; it is the acknowledgement of the Giver and His gracious will and favor

---

104 Peters, *The Lord's Prayer*, 119.

toward us in Christ. It is only through Christ that daily bread can be confessed as a gift. Disciples are praying in this petition that their eyes might be open to the bountiful goodness of the Father, who in Christ provides "everything that has to do with the supports and needs of the body." God is not unmindful of creaturely, physical, and social necessities such as "food, drink, clothing, shoes, house, home, land, animals, money, goods, a devout husband or wife, devout children, devout workers, devout and faithful rulers, good government, good weather, peace, health, self-control, good reputation, good friends, faithful neighbors, and the like." Disciples are not super-human and beyond the need for these necessities. Jesus would not have us believe that it is beneath our dignity as disciples to pray for these things that seem less than spiritual. The Fourth Petition is the recognition that "every good gift and every perfect gift is from above, coming down from the Father of lights, with whom there is no variation or shadow due to change" (James 1:16–17).

Oswald Bayer has described Luther's ethic as an "ethic of gift." Bayer observes that contrary to the prevalent view in the late Medieval Era, where one's relationship with God was based on an exchange wherein God's blessings were conditional on human action, Luther begins with the "conception of an open-handed, generous and incessantly giving God."[105] God's giving is not conditioned by our response. In the face of our stinginess, greed, and unbelief, He remains the Giver who freely causes His rain to drench the fields of those who do not know Him and His sunlight to warm the crops of idolaters. It is by faith that disciples receive daily bread as a divine gift and thus answer the Giver in thanksgiving.

Just as God provided manna to the children of Israel in the wilderness each day, forbidding them to hoard it up to consume later, Luther reminds disciples that we are to look to the Father for every good thing, trusting in His provisions rather than

---

105    Oswald Bayer, "The Ethics of Gift": 452.

consuming ourselves with anxiety or imprisoning our souls with worry.[106] Disciples live in the freedom of faith, for they know that the God who cares for them today will provide for the future, unknown though it may be.

## THE FIFTH PETITION

Such freedom is found in the forgiveness of sins. The Fifth Petition serves as perpetual penitential prayer, for even though disciples belongs to Christ, "we daily sin much and surely deserve nothing but punishment." In the Large Catechism, Luther stresses this point even more boldly, noting that this petition

> should serve God's purpose to break our pride and keep us humble. He has reserved to himself this prerogative: those who boast of their goodness and despise others should examine themselves and put this petition uppermost in their mind. They will find that they are no more righteous than anyone else, that in the presence of God all people must fall on their knees and be glad that we can come to forgiveness. Let none think that they will ever in this life reach the point where they do not need this forgiveness. In short, unless God constantly forgives, we are lost.

> (LC III 90–91; K-W, 452)

**The life of the disciple subsists in the forgiveness of sins.**

The forgiveness of sins is not merely the first step of the Christian life from which the disciple then climbs to ever higher rungs of the ladder. The life of the disciple subsists in the forgiveness of

---

106    Helmut Thielicke reminds us, "The Lord's Prayer teaches us to pray, not only for bread in general, but for *daily* bread, that is for the 'ration' that we need 'today.' . . . Even 'tomorrow' with its own cares (Matthew 6:34) is to be left in his hands; we are not to worry about what it will bring, but rather to cultivate the certainty that it does come from God's hands," in *Our Heavenly Father*, 87–88.

sins; it is not a preliminary platform that our sanctification allows us to move beyond. "This forgiveness," Luther says, "is not to be expected only at one time, as in baptism, as the Novatians teach, but frequently, as often as one needs it, till death" (AE 37:368). It is always needed, for without forgiveness of sins there is no life or communion with God, and so disciples pray the Fifth Petition without ceasing.

Forgiven by their Lord, disciples forgive one another in the way of Colossians 3:13: "Bearing with one another and, if one has a complaint against another, forgiving each other; as the Lord has forgiven you, so you also must forgive." Living in the constancy of God's forgiveness of our sins for the sake of Christ, disciples now practice that forgiveness in their life together. "God's forgiveness gives us sinners the power and freedom to practice forgiveness among one another."[107] Where the Lord's forgiveness has its way with us, absolving us from the enormity of our debt before God, we cannot stingily withhold from our neighbor the very gift of pardon that we have received without any worthiness on our part.

The petition is clean and clear. We are not taught to pray only to forgive the trespasses of those who repent of their offenses against us. Jesus' words are stark and to the point: "And forgive us our trespasses as we forgive those who trespass against us." In one sense, this is a devastating petition in that it brings us to humility, demonstrating that we have no claim to withhold forgiveness from those who sin against us, for the God who justifies the ungodly has not withheld His forgiveness from us, even though "we are neither worthy of the things for which we pray, nor have we deserved them . . . for we daily sin much and surely deserve nothing but punishment."

The Fifth Petition puts disciples in their place. They are both forgiven and forgiving. By faith, we receive God's forgiveness, and in love we forgive those who sin against us. Such is the way of discipleship. Reconciled to God in Christ, disciples are reconciled

---

107    Peters, *The Lord's Prayer*, 148.

to one another in this same Lord. Luther sees this petition as a consoling and outward sign of the fact that we are forgiven before God. This sign, the forgiveness that we extend to the neighbor, also comforts us with the knowledge that we are forgiven by Christ.[108]

# The Sixth Petition

The petition for the forgiveness of sins is coupled with the plea of the Sixth Petition: "And lead us not into temptation." Disciples are not exempt from temptation; from the satanic attack directed against the First Commandment. The target of the evil one is faith itself. Through seduction and deception, he promotes the lie that the Creator cannot be trusted and so would lead the disciple away from the Gospel and into "false belief, despair, and other great shame and vice." Entrapped by enticements into unbelief, one is brought to despair and, out of this hopelessness, is given over to the shameful works of the flesh in an attempt to find life but securing only death.

In the Large Catechism, Luther parses out the three categories of temptation: from the flesh, the world, and the devil.

New Testament scholar Udo Schnelle characterizes the life according to the flesh as "a life without access to God, a life that is captive to what is earthly and perishable."[109] The life of the flesh is helplessly organized around its own desires and so inevitably leads to death, even though it appears to be affirming of freedom and fulfillment.

The flesh is the "old creature" that we carry "around our necks" (LC III 102; K-W, 454), who "lures us daily into unchastity, laziness, gluttony and drunkenness, greed and deceit, into acts of fraud and deception against our neighbor" (LC III 102;

---

108    "For whatever baptism and the Lord's Supper, which are appointed to us as outward signs, can effect, this sign can as well, in order to strengthen and gladden our conscience. Moreover, above and beyond the other signs, it has been instituted precisely so that we can use and practice in every hour, keeping it with us at all times" (LC III 98; K-W, 453).

109    Udo Schnelle, *The Human Condition: Anthropology in the Teachings of Jesus, Paul, and John,* trans. O. C. Dean Jr. (Minneapolis: Fortress Press, 1991), 61.

K-W, 454). These are what the Scriptures call "the works of the flesh" (see Galatians 5:19–21). These carnal works are antithetical to the "ethic of gift" that we noted earlier; they center in the self, taking for themselves not what God has given but what He forbids. As such, their end is not life but death. The temptations of the flesh promise pleasure but give pain; they offer momentary delight but plunge into destruction.

The world is listed next. As Luther understands the world, it is the fallen creation that is darkened by sin, under the power of its prince (the evil one), and at enmity with its Creator. In contrast with the sphere of discipleship, "the world has become hardened by its own unbelief."[110] The "world" in this sense is not to be confused with the created cosmos, but with all that stands in opposition to God and His disciples.[111] Luther describes the dynamic of the world's alluring but toxic role in temptation:

> [It] assails us by word and deed and drives us to anger and impatience. In short, there is in it nothing but hatred and envy, enmity, violence and injustice, perfidy, vengeance, cursing, reviling, slander, arrogance, and pride, along with fondness for luxury, honor, fame, and power. For no one is willing to be the least, but everyone wants to sit on top and be seen by all.
>
> (LC III 103; K-W, 454)

Luther well knew the words of James "that friendship with the world is enmity with God" (James 4:4). Although it poses itself with masks of prestige and postures itself with power, the world with its allurements is passing and transitory (1 John 2:15–17).

The final member of this triad is "the devil, who baits and badgers us on all sides, but especially exerts himself where the conscience and spiritual matters are concerned" (LC III 104;

---

110     Udo Schnelle, *Theology of the New Testament*, 684.

111     Here see the discussion in Bruce Schuchard, *1–3 John*, Concordia Commentary (St. Louis: Concordia Publishing House, 2012), 223–26.

K-W, 454). To borrow the words of Heiko Oberman,[112] human life is lived "between God and the devil." The evil one does not rest from his diabolical attempts to separate the disciple from Christ, so he assaults the conscience, implanting doubt and seeking to convince the Christian that the promises of the Gospel are not for him or her. "At the heart of the Devil's strategy lies his ability to create confusion between law and gospel."[113] In this way, the devil aims to introduce uncertainty, unsettling the heart, substituting terror in the place of peace. Volker Leppin accurately pinpoints Luther's conviction:

> The temptation, the devil's pronouncing of the law instead of the gospel, is strongly connected in Luther's teaching on justification. The devil questions nothing less than exactly this delightful preaching of God, which endows us with salvation by grace alone, through faith alone. In the devil's temptations, the savior Christ is made into a judge, and human beings, saved believers, are made into hated persons and objects of accusation.[114]

The devil lives up to his biblical nomenclature; he is both accuser and murderer.

Luther sees temptation as a power that is too great for disciples to battle on the strength of their own powers. They need a deliverer who will rescue them from the enemy. Christ alone is the One who has achieved victory over the devil for us. The Sixth Petition then is a plea for the persistence of faith that the disciple might

---

112    See Heiko Oberman, *Luther: Man between God and the Devil,* trans. Eileen Walliser-Schwarzbart (New Haven: Yale University Press, 1989). Here also note the observation of Robert Kolb: "By his very nature, Satan is a liar, and through his lies he takes genuine life away from God's human creatures. The battle that climaxed in Christ's cross and tomb and that comes to conclusion only in the eschaton was continuing every day in the lives of all believers. Truth and deceit, God and the devil, are locked in constant combat, and believers must rely on the 'sword of the Spirit,'" in *Enduring Word,* 73.

113    Carl R. Trueman, *Luther on the Christian Life: Cross and Freedom* (Wheaton: Crossway Books, 2015), 128.

114    Volker Leppin, "Luther on the Devil," in *Encounters with Luther: New Directions for Critical Studies,* ed. Kirsi I. Stjerna and Brooks Schramm (Louisville: Westminster/John Knox, 2016), 35.

indeed persevere in Christ, who is for us in every way. Luther is once again completely realistic:

**The Sixth Petition then is a plea for the persistence of faith that the disciple might indeed persevere.**

> Every Christian must endure such great, grievous perils and attacks—grievous enough even if they come one at a time. As long as we remain in this vile life, where we are attacked, hunted, and harried on all sides, we are constrained to cry out and pray every hour that God may not allow us to become faint and weary and to fall back into sin, shame, and unbelief. Otherwise it is impossible to overcome even the smallest attack.

(LC III 105; K-W, 454)

"And lead us not into temptation" is a prayer of resistance that relies on Christ, who came into the flesh to destroy the works of the devil, works that are lodged in the conscience, which becomes his playground.

## THE SEVENTH PETITION

The flip side of the Sixth Petition, "And lead us not into temptation," is the Seventh Petition, "But deliver us from evil." Both of these petitions are prayed against the devil.

> It seems to be speaking of the devil as the sum of all evil in order that the entire substance of our prayer may be directed against our archenemy. For it is he who obstructs everything for which we ask: God's name or honor, God's kingdom and will, our daily bread, a good and cheerful conscience, etc.

(LC III:113; K-W, 455)

Evil is destructive of all that God calls good, but it is not merely a nameless, anti-godly power; it resides in the person of the evil one who opposes God's works and ways, restlessly seeking to overturn God's gifts and bring chaos into creation. Neither the Scriptures nor Luther understands the devil dualistically. Unlike God, the devil is not eternal, nor is his evil proportionate to God's goodness. Evil and the evil one do persist in this fallen creation, but God has set limits on the scope of evil.[115] The devil will finally be banished to hell forever, as he is already defeated by Christ and judged as the liar that he is (see John 16:11).

> **As disciples await the final victory, they continue to pray, "Deliver us from evil."**

As disciples await the final victory, they continue to pray, "Deliver us from evil" as it summarizes all that we ask for in the Lord's Prayer, namely, that "our Father in heaven would rescue us from every evil of body and soul, possessions and reputation, and finally, when our last hour comes, give us a blessed end, and graciously take us from this valley of sorrow to Himself in heaven."

Disciples pray the Seventh Petition out of the depths. Luther gives hymnic expression to this in stanza 1 of "From Depths of Woe I Cry to Thee":

> From depths of woe I cry to Thee,
>     In trial and tribulation;
> Bend down Thy gracious ear to me,
>     Lord, hear my supplication.
> If Thou rememb'rest every sin,
> Who then could heaven ever win
>     Or stand before Thy presence?
>
> (*LSB* 607:1)

---

115    Here see Hans Schwarz: "Evil remains among us as something very much alive and deeply threatening and destructive. Ultimately, evil is that which is antigodly, that is, it is that which experiences its limits and rejections through God, the source of all that is good.... God himself has set boundaries for evil that it cannot overstep," in *Evil: A Historical and Theological Perspective* (Minneapolis: Fortress Press, 1995), 211. Also note Oswald Bayer: "As evil is denied in God's 'very good' creation (Gen. 1:31), so it will be overcome in the eschaton, with the consummation of my own life-story and with the consummation of world history," in "Does Evil Persist?" *Lutheran Quarterly* 11 (1997): 143.

Our neediness in the face of evil—both physical and spiritual—drive us to pray, running to the Father rather than running away from Him. Jonah becomes an example of one who prays "deliver us from evil," as Luther notes,

> For there was nothing else to do in such need of both body and soul but cry out. Our desires, our powers are nothing, just as Jonah here called out in pressing need. No merit was present, for he had sinned very seriously against the Lord. And so the only thing to do was to cry out, to cry out "to the Lord." For the Lord is the only one to whom we must flee as to a sacred anchor and the only safety on those occasions when we think that we are done for.
>
> (AE 19:16–17)

## THE CONCLUSION

Perhaps the hardest part of learning to pray as disciples is learning how to say "Amen." Prayer for disciples of Jesus Christ begins and ends with faith. We pray with all boldness and confidence because our Father has invited us to believe that "He is our true Father and that we are His true children." This knowledge gives us the certainty that our petitions are pleasing to our Father and are heard by Him. This knowledge is anchored on a twofold truth. God has commanded us to pray in this way and He has promised to hear us.[116]

---

116 Here see Mary Jane Haemig: "He [Luther] asserted that Christians pray because God has commanded them to pray and promised to hear them. For this reason, Christians pray to God, not to Mary or the saints. Prayer was the proper response to God; it never originated the relationship with God. Luther rejected the idea that prayer was a good work and rejected practices—such as the repletion of prayers and the use of prayers for works of satisfaction—that might lend support to the idea that prayer was a good work. Prayer was not based on the Christian's worthiness to pray. Need drives her to pray, and she brings all her needs to God, trusting God's promise to hear her. As every Christian is a priest, every Christian should pray. One should not trust in others' prayers and should not leave prayer to the clergy. Prayer should come from the heart and be simple," in "Jehoshaphat and His Prayer among Sixteenth-Century Lutherans," in *Church History* 73 (2004): 524. As we shall see in chapter 8, Luther anchors the practice of daily prayer in the confidence that we may speak to God because He has given us His name.

Prayer is not simply a repetitive ritual done with the attitude that it might be more or less pleasing to God. To be a Christian is to pray. This command "defined the Christian life."[117] But God's unrelenting command alone is not sufficient to evoke prayer, for as Wengert elucidates, "A true Christian was someone who had been worked over by the law and driven to the gospel."[118] Neither our desperate need nor the strict demand of the Law can produce God-pleasing prayer. It is only when the word of promise is added to the command that we disciples can call God our Father with devotion and delight in the way described in the Small Catechism. "Amen" is the signature of faith that lives with the confidence that God has not only commanded us to pray in this way but has, in His Son, also promised to hear us. "God has attached much importance to our being certain so that we do not pray in vain or despise our prayers in any way" (LC III 124; K-W, 456).

**To be a Christian is to pray.**

The "Amen" of faith does not signal the disciple's withdrawal from the world, with its disappointments and causes for despair, but perseverance in the confidence that the God to whom we pray governs our days and deeds in His mercy.[119]

---

117    Timothy J. Wengert, "Luther on Prayer in the Large Catechism," in *The Pastoral Luther: Essays on Martin Luther's Practical Theology*, ed. Timothy J. Wengert (Grand Rapids: Eerdmans, 2009), 188.

118    Wengert, "Luther on Prayer in the Large Catechism," 188.

119    Here see Gustaf Wingren: "To await help from the Lord means not turning aside before adversities and forsaking one's vocation, but continuing in faith and prayer," in *Luther on Vocation*, 189.

*For Further Reflection and Study: Connections with Luther's Small Catechism with Explanation 2017*

1. How does the conclusion of each article of the Creed with the words "This is most certainly true" form the basis for prayer? (See p. 231.)

2. What place does prayer have in the life of a disciple? (See pp. 232–36.)

3. Why to do we call God "our Father"? (See pp. 237–39.)

4. How is the First Petition connected to the Second Commandment? (See pp. 242–43.)

5. In the Second Article of the Creed, we are taught that Jesus has redeemed us that we might live under Him in His kingdom. What are the characteristics of this kingdom of God? (See pp. 247–48.) How does this kingdom come to us? (See pp. 247–51.)

6. How do we know the will of God? (See pp. 253–54, 256.)

7. How is the will of Satan opposed to God's will? (See pp. 254–255.)

8. If God gives daily bread even without our prayer, why do we pray for it? (See pp. 258–261.)

9. How does God's forgiveness determine the way we deal with those who sin against us? (See pp. 264–68.)

10. What are the three sources of temptation? (See pp. 271.)

11. What are the promises of God in the face of temptation? (See pp. 271–72.)

12. How is the Seventh Petition as summary of the entire Lord's Prayer? (See pp. 274–76.)

13. How is the Seventh Petition a prayer against Satan? (See pp. 276–78.)

14. Where did the Conclusion of the Lord's Prayer come from? (See pp. 279–80.)

15. What does the word "Amen" confess? (See p. 280.)

——▸·:•——•:·◂——

# Chapter 5

# Holy Baptism:
# How Disciples Are Made and Kept

> Therefore faith is not a laughable, cold quality that
> snores and is idle in the heart. No it is agitated and
> harassed by horrible trials concerning the nothingness
> and the vanity of the divine promises. For I believe in
> Christ, whom I do not see. But I have His Baptism,
> the Sacrament of the Altar, and consolation through
> the Word and Absolution. Yet I see nothing of what
> He promises. Indeed, I feel the opposite in my flesh.
> Here, then, one must struggle and do battle against
> unbelief and doubt.
>
> MARTIN LUTHER, *LECTURES ON GALATIANS*
> *(CHAPTERS 26–30)* (AE 5:205)

Water, water everywhere but not a drop to drink," said the poet Coleridge. God, God everywhere but not a Savior in sight. Luther said God is in the rope but you'll hang yourself if you try to find Him there, and that God is in the ocean but you'll drown if you seek to discover Him there. God's presence is elusive, for as the prophet Isaiah says, He is a God who hides Himself (see Isaiah 45:15).

God is omnipresent. There is not an inch of the universe where He is not present, sustaining and upholding His creation. God being everywhere present is not the Gospel. He is present also in

His wrath working death and destruction. The scenic mountain stream, with its swift currents, has the power to suck a hapless fisherman underneath its currents to a watery death. God is hidden in the water, quenching the thirst of human beings and animals, causing gardens to flourish and deserts to become lush fields. This same God is hidden in the hurricanes, whose indiscriminate waves sweep away villages. You won't get very far meditating on water. There is no certainty in the water whether it be a gentle stream or a raging river. From the water, you will never know whether God is for you or against, whether He is friend or foe. Baptism does not lead us to ponder the wetness of the water but to cling to the Word of God in the water.

> ━━✦┈✦━━✦┈╋━
> **Baptism does not lead us to ponder the wetness of the water but to cling to the Word of God in the water.**
> ━━✦┈✦━━✦┈╋━

# FIRST

## *WHAT IS BAPTISM?*

The Word of God that is in the water is not just any word but a specific word of promise.[120] In his initial Baptismal sermon on Pentecost, Peter preached that promise from Joel: "And it shall come to pass that everyone who calls on the name of the Lord shall be saved" (Acts 2:21). It is that name of the Lord into which we are baptized, as the risen Jesus sends His apostles to make disciples by "baptizing them in the name of the Father and of the Son and of the Holy Spirit."[121] Baptism is not an ecclesiastical

---

120    Here see Steven Paulson: "The word that is put into the water is not a general word, but a specific one: a promise given to us. That word is by Christ's command: 'Go therefore and make disciples of all nations, baptizing them in the name of the Father and of the Son and of the Holy Spirit' (Matt. 28:19). In this word, God bestows his name by proclaiming it out loud (fulfilling the third commandment in which an unholy thing becomes holy) and so fulfilling the second commandment to keep the name holy by grasping it. The name is given so that we may call upon the Lord on the final day, just as Joel promised—a promise that Paul extended over to the Gentiles: 'Everyone who calls on the name of the Lord shall be saved' (Romans 10:13; Joel 2:32)," in "Graspable God," *Word & World* (Winter 2012): 54. Also recall Luther's words in the Genesis lectures: "In Baptism the voice of the Trinity is heard" (AE 8:145).

121    On Jesus' instituting of Holy Baptism in Matthew 28, see Robert Kolb, "Holy Baptism," in *Confessing the Gospel,*

custom that may or may not be observed according to the will or circumstances of Christians. "Baptism is not the changeable initiation rite of a religious fellowship but an unalterable sacrament of our Lord Jesus Christ. Consequently the will, command, and fancy of men do not provide the basis for this Sacrament, but only the institution of Christ."[122] Now "Baptism is not just plain water, but it is the water included in God's command and combined with God's word."

God's Word makes Baptism what it is.[123] Separated from the Word of God, the water is no different than the water that runs out of a tap in your kitchen. It would be a mere "bath-keeper's baptism," to use the words of the Large Catechism. Baptism is such a great and precious jewel because it is there that the Lord has located His promise. What does He promise? "Whoever believes and is baptized shall be saved." Baptized in the name of the Father and of the Son and of the Holy Spirit, we are given His name to call upon. Everyone who calls upon this name shall be saved. Baptism demonstrates that God does not deal with us from the heights of His heavenly majesty but condescends to us, locating Himself by plunging His Word into water.[124]

Disciples of Jesus know that Baptism is not an ordinance of the Law, a legal requirement to be complied with in order to be qualified for salvation. It is to be understood evangelically as promise and gift. "Baptism is not merely something instituted

---

754–57, especially his discussion of the triune name that "implies that through Baptism Christians are brought into the closest relationship with the only true God. They bear on their bodies the marks of God. They have become his possession and are under his protection and control" (757). Also see Norman E. Nagel, "Holy Baptism," in *Lutheran Worship: History and Practice*, ed. Fred Precht (St. Louis: Concordia Publishing House, 1993), 262–89, especially his discussion of the Lord's mandate: "The Lord's triune name comes first in Holy Baptism. If he had not given us his name we would still be making up our own gods. His is the initiative; the action is from him to us. 'In the name' means— along with much more—at his bidding, by his authority, his mandate" (262). See also Edmund Schlink, "The Baptismal Command" in *The Doctrine of Baptism*, trans. Herbert J. A. Bouman (St. Louis: Concordia Publishing House, 1972), 9–12.

122    Hermann Sasse, "Circular Letter 4 to Westphalian Pastors: Holy Baptism," in *Letters to Lutheran Pastors: vol. 1. 1948–1951*, ed. Matthew C. Harrison (St. Louis: Concordia Publishing House, 2013), 462–63.

123    See Hermann Sasse: "All effects of Baptism are effects of the Word combined with the water for Luther and the Lutheran Church," in "Holy Baptism" in *Letters to Lutheran Pastors*, vol. 1, ed. Matthew C. Harrison (St. Louis: Concordia Publishing House, 2013), 61.

124    Here see Peters: "The triune God does not deal with us in Baptism only from the heights of His majesty; Word and element are saturated at the same time with what He did when He turned to us in love," in *Commentary on Luther's Catechism: Baptism and Lord's Supper*, trans. Thomas Trapp (St. Louis: Concordia Publishing House, 2012), 93.

by God as a legal demand, but it is at the same time primarily God's grace-filled promise, which is complete in itself, taken hold by us in faith, and which is to be held onto firmly."[125] Baptism is not our ladder to climb up into God's presence but His coming to us in mercy and grace. Luther captures this most pointedly in stanzas 4 and 7 of his catechetical hymn "To Jordan Came the Christ, Our Lord":

> There stood the Son of God in love,
> His grace to us extending;
> The Holy Spirit like a dove
> Upon the scene descending;
> The triune God assuring us,
> With promises compelling
> That in our Baptism He will thus
> Among us find a dwelling
> To comfort and sustain us.
>
> All that the mortal eye beholds
> Is water as we pour it.
> Before the eye of faith unfolds
> The pow'r of Jesus' merit.
> For here it sees the crimson flood
> To all our ills bring healing;
> The wonders of His precious blood
> The love of God revealing,
> Assuring His own pardon.
>
> (*LSB* 407:4, 7; © 1976 Elizabeth Quitmeyer)

# Second

### *What Benefits Does Baptism Give?*

With His Word in the water, Jesus gives you the benefits of His redeeming death. We are reminded of this in the baptismal

---

125   Peters, *Baptism and Lord's Supper*, 97.

liturgy, when the pastor says, "Receive the sign of the holy cross both upon your forehead and upon your heart to mark you as one redeemed by Christ the crucified" (*LSB*, p. 268) as he traces the cross on the head and chest of the one brought to Baptism. In the explanation of the Creed's Second Article, we confess that Jesus, true God and true man, "has redeemed me, a lost and condemned person, purchased and won me from all sins, from death, and from the power of the devil; not with gold or silver, but with His holy, precious blood and with His innocent suffering and death." Now that work of Christ for you is given to you in Baptism, where "it works forgiveness of sins, rescues from death and the devil, and gives eternal salvation to all who believe this, as the words and promises of God declare."

To say "I am baptized" is to say "Jesus died for me." This is what the words and promises of God declare. You belong to Him, for He died to snatch you out of the grasp of those tyrants and kidnappers—sin, which would enslave; the devil, who accuses your conscience; and death, which strips you of life with God. In Baptism, He has put His name on you. You belong to Him and have His promise: "everyone who calls on the name of the Lord shall be saved" (Joel 2:32; Romans 10:13). The waters of Baptism are soon dried, but this promise of God will never evaporate for the Word of the Lord endures forever. Listen to the Large Catechism: "Thus you see plainly that baptism is not a work that we do but that it is a treasure that God gives us and faith grasps, just as the Lord Christ upon the cross is not a work but a treasure placed in the setting of the Word and offered to us in the Word and received by faith" (LC IV 37; K-W, 461). To live in your Baptism is to trust that Word in life and in death.

> **The waters of Baptism are soon dried, but this promise of God will never evaporate.**

The Lord who has purchased and won us by His Passion now claims us as His own possession in Baptism. Edmund Schlink puts it like this:

> Being assigned to Jesus Christ, the Lord, as His property, this is being placed under the present rule of the Crucified comes to the baptized as something done to him. Just as Christian Baptism is not a self-Baptism but a being baptized, so the baptized does not become Christ's property by placing *himself* under Christ, but rather *becomes* Christ's property through Baptism. This is God's deed; this is acceptance by the Lord.[126]

This deed is done by the triune God as His Word is enclosed in the water to accomplish His saving purpose, namely, to reclaim lives who were dead in their trespasses and sins. Baptism is God's action.

Sadly, much of American Christianity sees Baptism as a kind of pledge of allegiance to Christ, the first act that the converted person engages in to declare his or her loyalty to the Savior. Karl Barth was perhaps the most articulate spokesman for this view. In his *Church Dogmatics*, he accents man's turning to the faithfulness of God and then asserts:

> The first step of this life of faithfulness to God, the Christian life, is a man's baptism with water, which by his own decision is requested of the community, as a binding confession of obedience, conversion, and hope, made in prayer for God's grace, wherein he honours the freedom of grace.[127]

---

126  Edmund Schlink, *The Doctrine of Baptism*, 44.

127  Karl Barth, *Church Dogmatics*, vol. 4, part 4, trans. G. W. Bromiley (Peabody, MA: Hendrickson Publishers, 2010), 2.

In his polemic against the Baptism of infants, Barth argued:

> **Christian baptism is in essence the representation of a man's renewal through his participation by means of the power of the Holy Spirit in the death and resurrection of Jesus Christ, and there with the representation of man's association with Christ, with the covenant of grace which is concluded and realized in Him, and with the fellowship of His Church.**[128]

# THIRD

### HOW CAN WATER DO SUCH GREAT THINGS?

Baptism with water is seen as symbolizing an internal, spiritual reality, not as actually delivering regeneration by the Holy Spirit. In this theology, Baptism becomes the disciple's initial act of obedience. For the New Testament and for Luther, Baptism is God's act of rescue and as such is the source and foundation for the life of discipleship, for in it we are born again of water and the Spirit (John 3:1–5) and so are saved (see 1 Peter 3:21).

Water can do great and mighty things. If you have witnessed the aftermath of a flood or hurricane, you know that. As you walked across mud-caked floors or waded through murky and swollen streams, you saw people whose lives were submerged in chaos and destruction. Water can do great things. It can be harnessed to produce electrical energy and irrigate parched wasteland; it can be channeled to create lakes for recreation, but water without the Word of God remains plain water with no power to give eternal life.

We have already heard how the Lord puts His Word in the water to give us His name and, in and with that name, all the

---

128    Karl Barth, *The Teaching of the Church Regarding Baptism,* trans. Ernest A. Payne (London: SCM Press, 1954), 9. For a decisive Lutheran critique of Barth's position, see Hermann Sasse, "Holy Baptism," 56–57.

benefits of Jesus' death: forgiveness of sins and rescue from death and the devil. Now in this third part of Holy Baptism, Luther unpacks it for us. It is not the water that does these great things "but the word of God in and with the water . . . along with the faith which trusts this word of God in the water." God locates Himself for us in Baptism, making a washing of regeneration. In a 1534 sermon, Luther proclaims,

> Thus we do not need to look elsewhere for the Spirit if we have the Sacrament of Baptism, since we have Christ's words and institution that the name of the Holy Spirit is present along with that of the Father and Son (that is, of the whole divine Majesty). And since God's name and Word are in it, you are not permitted to regard it as plain and simple water that does no more than bathwater, but rather the kind of water by which we are cleansed from sin and, as the Scripture calls it, a washing of regeneration [Titus 3:5] by which we are reborn into eternal life.[129]

Jesus says of marriage that what God has joined together, man is not to put asunder. So it is with Baptism. The Word of God is in the water, and where that Word is, there is the Spirit. Word and Spirit together—not the Word down here and the Spirit off in the heavenly regions who might flutter in from time to time. "By the word of the LORD the heavens were made, and by the breath of His mouth all their host" (Psalm 33:6) says the psalmist.

The Spirited-word in the water is doing the deed. Baptism is not the work of human beings but of God. No more than you could create yourself can you re-create yourself, you are not the source of your own genesis, and you are not the source of your own regeneration. Say what you will about the necessity of being born again, but you can't pull that off any more than you could

---

129    "Sermons on Holy Baptism 1534," in *Martin Luther on Holy Baptism: Sermons to the People (1525–39)*, ed. Benjamin T. G. Mayes (St. Louis: Concordia Publishing House, 2018), 27.

have been the cause of your own birth. It is the work of the Father, who has saved you through this washing of rebirth and renewal poured out on you by the Holy Spirit through Jesus Christ, His own Son. Luther's citation of Paul's words to Titus echo what was promised by the Lord through the prophet Ezekiel: "I will sprinkle clean water on you, and you shall be clean from all your uncleannesses, and from all your idols I will cleanse you. And I will give you a new heart, and a new spirit I will put within you" (Ezekiel 36:25–26).

The Word of God in the water makes Baptism "a life-giving water, rich in grace, and a washing of rebirth in the Holy Spirit." Dead in our trespasses and sins, we could not come to God, much less render Him the gift of the old rusty tin can of our heart, to paraphrase the old rector in Bo Giertz's *The Hammer of God*. The Catechism confesses, "I believe that I cannot by my own reason or strength believe in Jesus Christ, my Lord, or come to Him; but the Holy Spirit has called me by the Gospel." This is what the Spirit is doing in Baptism. He is bringing life out of death, righteousness out of sin, a new creation out of nothingness. "If anyone is in Christ, he is a new creation. The old has passed away; behold, the new has come" (2 Corinthians 5:17). Such is the miracle of your Baptism.

What God has joined together, man is not to separate. God has bound Word and Spirit together. Baptism and faith are joined together. It is the Word of God in the water doing these great things of forgiving sin and rescuing from death and the devil. And it is faith that trusts this Word of God in the water. Luther describes Baptism like this in the Large Catechism: "it is a treasure that God gives us and faith grasps" (LC IV 37; K-W, 461). Faith does not make Baptism what it is, but it is only through faith that we receive the blessings of Baptism. Luther observes, "Faith is not there for the sake of Baptism, but Baptism is there for the sake of faith."[130] Baptism gives faith something to believe in.[131]

---

130    Cited by Peters in *Baptism and Lord's Supper*, 103.

131    See Gerhard Forde, "Something to Believe: A Theological Perspective on Infant Baptism," in *The Preached God:*

This faith is not of your own making. It is not a decision that you have made for Christ. It is not a commitment that you have conjured up to demonstrate your sincerity in following Christ. It is trust in the promises of Christ Jesus to be your Lord. Baptism does give you something to believe in: Christ with all His gifts for you. Listen again to the Large Catechism:

> **Baptism does give you something to believe in: Christ with all His gifts for you.**

In Baptism, therefore, every Christian has enough to study and practice all his or her life. Christians always have enough to do to believe firmly what baptism promises and brings—victory over death and the devil, forgiveness of sin, God's grace, the entire Christ, and the Holy Spirit with his gifts.

(LC IV 41–42; K-W, 461)

If one views discipleship as an act of the human will, a decision that one makes to follow Jesus, the Baptism of infants becomes problematic. But if we recognize that sin extends over the whole of humanity and Christ's atonement is for the sins of the whole world to be received by faith, then the baptizing of infants is set in a new light.

> We baptize children as if they were adults, just as we baptize adults as if they were children. Whatever the differences between adults and children may mean for us humans and our judgment of a person, it means nothing for God. Before Him a person is a person, either a child of Adam or a child of God, regardless of age.[132]

---

*Proclamation in Word and Sacrament*, ed. Mark C. Mattes and Steven D. Paulson (Grand Rapids: Eerdmans, 2007), 131–45.

132    Sasse, "Holy Baptism," 65. For more on the Baptism of infants, see Kolb, "Holy Baptism," in *Confessing the Gospel*, 780–84. For Luther on the Baptism of infants, see "Infant Baptism and Faith That Is Not One's Own" (1525), in *Martin Luther on Holy Baptism: Sermons to the People (1525–1539)*, 3–12.

After an overly zealous Karlstadt had nearly turned the Reformation into a revolution, Luther returned to Wittenberg and preached his "Invocavit Sermons" in 1522. In the first of these sermons, Luther spoke words that are as stunning as they are sober:

> The summons of death comes to us all, and no one can die for another. Every one must fight his own battle with death by himself alone. We can shout into another's ears, but every one must himself be prepared for the time of death, for I will not be with you then, nor you with me.
>
> (AE 51:70)

Then Luther said: "Therefore every one must himself know and be armed with the chief things which concern a Christian" (AE 51:70). What are these chief things that concern a Christian? They are the stuff of the Catechism—the Ten Commandments, the Creed, the Lord's Prayer, and the Sacraments.

Baptism is there. It is a chief thing for the Christian, for it is there, in the water "included in God's command and combined with God's Word," that the Spirit works the forgiveness of sins, delivers from death and the devil to all who believe this as the words and promises of God declare. There we find "our only comfort and the doorway to all of God's possessions and to the communion of all the saints" as Luther puts it in his *Baptismal Booklet* (K-W, 373).

# FOURTH

### *WHAT DOES SUCH BAPTIZING WITH WATER INDICATE?*

Luther's intention is not simply that we know about Baptism but rather that we know how to live in our Baptism, daily dying and drowning all sins and evil desires and daily coming to live before God in righteousness and purity forever. Perhaps the most unique thing about Luther's catechetical treatment of Baptism when compared with the medieval tradition was this fourth part of Baptism:"What does such baptizing with water indicate?" That's another way of asking, What does Baptism have to do with my life, my daily life in this world?

Baptism is not a ceremony that we now see only in the rearview mirror. It is not just "I *was* baptized, but I *am* baptized." Baptism is present tense. Much more than an awe-inspiring rite of initiation, Baptism is incorporation into the death of Jesus Christ for your sin and sharing in that death; you now live by the promise of His resurrection.

> **Baptism is not a ceremony that we now see only in the rearview mirror.**

The Christian life is one of getting used to your Baptism. To be baptized is to be put to death. "Do you not know," says the apostle, "that all of us who have been baptized into Christ Jesus were baptized into His death? (Romans 6:3). The death Jesus died, He died for sin. Yours is not a death for sin but a death to sin. This means death to the old Adam. "So you also must consider yourselves dead to sin and alive to God in Christ Jesus" (Romans 6:11). The old Adam does not sink like a heavy anchor into the sea. He is a swimmer and a muscular one at that. Always poking his head up, gasping for yet another breath of lethal life. His is never an easy death! The old Adam never passes away quietly or peacefully.

This means that you never outgrow contrition and repentance. The Catechism describes it as a daily death. Death is the rhythm of the Christian's life all the way through to the resurrection of the body. Only when this body has died will you be through with death. Then there will be no more old Adam, only a new man who will live with God and without sin in righteousness and purity forever. But now in this life, the old man remains, and there is no way for him to peacefully coexist with the new man. He can suffer only death, death that comes by contrition and repentance as you put your Amen to God's work of breaking and hindering every evil plan and purpose of the devil, the world, and yes, especially your own sinful nature, which does not want you to hallow God's name or let His kingdom come.

Baptismal clichés have attached themselves to our speaking like barnacles on the hull of a ship. One of those clichés is "Remember your Baptism." For the apostle Paul and for Luther, the admonition to remember your Baptism is not an invitation to recollect in your mind a picture of an idyllic gathering of family and friends around a font, but a battle cry to count yourself dead to sin and alive to God in Christ Jesus. It is a call to repent and believe the good news that the life you now live you live by faith in the Son of God, who loved you and gave Himself up for you. It is the call to keep crawling back to your Baptism and there to call upon the name of the Lord, trusting in the promise that you will be saved. The Lord who makes the promise is faithful and true: "We were buried therefore with Him by baptism into death, in order that, just as Christ was raised from the dead by the glory of the Father, we too might walk in newness of life" (Romans 6:4).[133]

To rightly remember your Baptism is to live from it and ever return to it. Because Baptism entails death and resurrection, it "marks the intersection of the old world and the new. Ethical progress is only possible by returning to Baptism."[134] Because Baptism endows us with Christ and all His gifts, sanctification is not a process that leads beyond Christ to a higher ontological perfection in this life but is a continual return to Baptism in repentance and faith. "Repentance, therefore, is nothing else than a return and approach to baptism, to resume and practice what has earlier been begun but abandoned" (LC IV 79; K-W, 466).

---

133    Here see Schlink: "Paul understood Baptism not only as assignment to the person of Jesus Christ but also as assignment to His history. Baptism into Christ is Baptism into His death. 'Do you not know that all of us who have been baptized into Christ Jesus were baptized into His death?' (Rom. 6:3). To be assigned to Christ is to be given into His death on the cross and into His grave. The Baptism event indeed takes place temporally removed from Jesus' death, but through Baptism the person is given into that death which Jesus Christ died once for all," in *The Doctrine of Baptism*, 47.

134    Oswald Bayer, *Living by Faith*, 66.

This is why Jonathan Trigg describes Luther's understanding of the Christian life as circular. "Conversion itself becomes, not an event, but a state to be preserved in by the Christian who must be *semper penitens*."[135] The Christian is always a penitent, perpetually returning to Baptism, where he or she is strengthened to live in faith toward Christ and in love toward the neighbor. This life, Trigg observes, "is no complacent reflection on past victories but an armed struggle."[136]

> **The Christian is always a penitent, perpetually returning to Baptism.**

In the Large Catechism, Luther speaks of progress, but this is not self-improvement. Luther writes instead of the Christian life as an ongoing Baptism:

> Thus a Christian life is nothing else than a daily baptism, begun once and continuing ever after. For we must keep at it without ceasing, always purging whatever pertains to the old Adam, so that whatever belongs to the new creature may come forth. What is the old creature? It is what is born in us from Adam, irascible, spiteful, envious, unchaste, greedy, lazy, proud—yes— and unbelieving; it is beset with all vices and by nature has nothing good in it. Now, when we enter Christ's kingdom, this corruption must daily decrease so that the longer we live the more gentle, patient, and meek we become, and the more we break away from greed, hatred, envy, and pride.
>
> (LC IV 66–67; K-W, 465)

Luther speaks not of the renovation of the old man, but of his death. The old Adam cannot be domesticated; he must daily be

---

135    Jonathan Trigg, *Baptism in the Theology of Martin Luther* (Leiden: Brill Academic Publisher, 1994), 170.

136    Trigg, 170. Also note Regin Prenter's description of this struggle: "Since sanctification is the practice of our baptismal faith in its struggle against the unbelief (the flesh) which constantly asserts itself after baptism, sanctification must have a twofold content: the constant suppression of the old man and the constant strengthening of the new man," in *Creation and Redemption,* trans. Theodor I. Jenson (Philadelphia: Fortress Press, 1967), 474.

put to death. It is only in this baptismal dying (repentance) that the new man comes forth to live before God in righteous and purity forever.

You cannot grow out of your Baptism, coming to that point where you no longer need it. The life of sanctification is not character formation but repentance and faith, death and resurrection:

> Therefore, learn that Baptism is nothing temporary, as the world sees it with carnal eyes, imagining that Baptism only avails once. But know that by Baptism you enter into an eternal covenant, and even if you sin, you have Baptism behind you. Go back into it. Christ does not fall from His throne even though you sin. Be afraid because you have fallen from Christ, but enter into the covenant again, and do not say, "I will take up a new order in which I will do many good works so that God will forgive my sin." No! You must return to the covenant of your Baptism and say, "I fell out of it, but I will take hold again of the ship that does not break apart." For the price is the kingdom of Christ, which is not lost on account of your fall.[137]

---

137   "Sermons on Holy Baptism (1538)," in *Martin Luther on Holy Baptism: Sermons to the People (1525–39)*, 97.

## For Further Reflection and Study: Connections with Luther's Small Catechism with Explanation 2017

1. Read Matthew 3:13–17 in light of Matthew 28:19–20. How are all three persons of the Trinity present in Jesus' Baptism? (See pp. 285–86.)

2. What is the significance of the Lord's name in Baptism? (See p. 287.)

3. Can infants be disciples? (See pp. 288–89.)

4. What makes Baptism sure and certain? (See pp. 290–91.)

5. What does the Lord give us in Baptism? (See pp. 292–93.)

6. How is faith connected to Baptism? (See pp. 294–96.)

7. Read John 3:1–15; how does the imagery of birth fit with Baptism? (See pp. 297–98.)

8. What does the Holy Spirit do in Baptism? (See pp. 298–300.)

9. What happens to the old Adam in Baptism? Read Romans 6:1–14. (See pp. 302–3.)

10. How is discipleship a continual return to Baptism? (See p. 302.)

## Chapter 6

———— +·:•—•:·+ ————

# Confession and Absolution: Disciples Live by the Forgiveness of Sins

I have a high regard for private confession, for here God's word and absolution are spoken privately and individually to each believer for the forgiveness of his sins, and as often as he desires it he may have recourse to it for this forgiveness, and also for comfort, counsel, and guidance. Thus it is a precious, useful thing for souls, as long as no one is driven to it with laws and commandments but sinners are left free to make use of it, each according to his own need.

MARTIN LUTHER, *CONFESSION CONCERNING CHRIST'S SUPPER*
(AE 37:368)

D isciples are not without sin. We have already observed that under the Fifth Petition of the Lord's Prayer, Luther has us pray continually for God's forgiveness because "we daily sin much and surely deserve nothing but punishment." The inclusion of material on Confession and Absolution between the chief parts of Holy Baptism and the Sacrament of the Altar was Luther's attempt to recognize this reality and provide comfort to disciples who are terrified by their sin and seek to struggle against it.

Luther realized that without confession and absolution, sinners will attempt in one way or another to deal with their own sins, making matters worse as they end up in either arrogance or despair, for the default mode of human existence is self-justification. We are apt at confessing the sins of others only to make ourselves look less culpable. We seek justification.

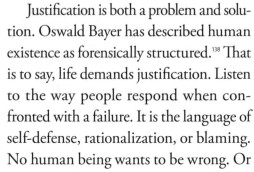

**Without confession and absolution, sinners will attempt in one way or another to deal with their own sins, making matters worse.**

Justification is both a problem and solution. Oswald Bayer has described human existence as forensically structured.[138] That is to say, life demands justification. Listen to the way people respond when confronted with a failure. It is the language of self-defense, rationalization, or blaming. No human being wants to be wrong. Or listen to the eulogies delivered at the memorial rites for unbelievers. They are, more often than not, attempts to vocalize why the deceased person's life was worthwhile. They seek to justify his or her existence. If one is not justified by faith in Christ, one will seek justification elsewhere in attitude or action.

To confess your sin is to cease the futile attempt to self-justify. Rather, it is to join with David in saying to God, "Against You, You only, have I sinned and done what is evil in Your sight, so that You might be justified in Your words and blameless in Your judgment" (Psalm 51:4). In confession, the sinner acknowledges that God is right. It is to agree with God's verdict: guilty.

But to speak of guilt requires some clarification today, for another word has come to attach itself to guilt. So we speak of guilt feelings. Guilt is seen as the subjective reaction of the doer to the deed, that is, how I feel about what I have done.[139] But this is not the case with the Scriptures' use of the word *guilt*. In the Bible, guilt has not so much to do with emotions as it does with what happens in a courtroom when a judge declares the defendant "guilty." The criminal may or may not have reactions of remorse, regret, or shame. It doesn't matter. The verdict of

---

138    See Oswald Bayer, *Living by Faith*, 1–9.

139    On this point, see the discussion of Werner Elert in *The Christian Ethos*, 163–73. Elert traces the subjective understanding of guilt to F. Schleiermacher.

the judge establishes the reality. God's word of Law unerringly establishes His judgment. There is no appeal.

To deny the verdict means that the truth is not in us, says the apostle John (see 1 John 1:8). But denial can never bring release. Only God's absolution can release from the accusation of the Law and unlock the sinner from his sins. Lutheran theology is nothing if it is not realistic![140] Like the Scriptures, Lutheran theology does not start with notions about human freedom and the potential (great or small) that human beings have. Theologies that start with assumptions about human freedom end up in bondage.[141] Lutheran theology begins with man's terrible bondage to sin and ends up with the glorious liberty of the Gospel. The bondage to sin is not a slight defect that can be corrected by appropriate self-discipline. Neither is it a sickness that can be cured by the appropriation of the medication of regular doses of God's grace. Sin is enmity with the Creator and carries with it God's verdict of guilt and a divinely imposed death sentence. To be a sinner is to be held captive in death and condemnation. The distance between God and humanity is not the gap between infinity and the finite but between a holy God, who is judge, and man, who is the guilty defendant.

> **Lutheran theology begins with man's terrible bondage to sin and ends up with the glorious liberty of the Gospel.**

Confession is the acknowledgment of this reality. So in a rite of individual Confession and Absolution based on Luther's order, we pray: "I, a poor sinner, plead guilty before God of all sins. I have lived as if God did not matter and as if I mattered most" (*LSB*, p. 292). The sin is named, not in an effort to "get it off my chest," but to acknowledge it before the Lord, to whom no secrets are hidden. Where sin is not confessed, it remains

---

140    Here note the German New Testament exegete Udo Schnelle's comment on Pauline anthropology: "His view of human beings is not merely pessimistic, but realistic," in *Theology of the New Testament*, 319.

141    See Gerhard Forde, *The Captivation of the Will* (Grand Rapids: Eerdmans, 2005), 21.

festering and corrosive, addicting the sinner to yet another go at self-justification. Confession admits defeat and so leaves the penitent open for a word that declares righteousness, a verdict that justifies. That word is *absolution*. It is absolution alone, says Gerhard Forde, that is the answer to the absolute claim of God, who is inescapably present to the sinner.[142]

The focus in Confession and Absolution is not on the confession per se, but on the Absolution.[143] Disconnected from the Absolution, confession turns into just another effort to save ourselves. Then the old Adam begins to reckon that he is right with God because his confession was so completely sincere or deeply heartfelt. Or that he has been so pious and courageous to make individual Confession a part of his regular spiritual discipline. In the Medieval Church, the requirement of no less than an annual trip to the confessional booth and the enumeration of specific sins had transformed confession into a spiritual torture chamber rather than an occasion for broken bones to be made glad in the Word from the Lord: "I forgive you all your sins." At this point, Luther filters the old practice of private Confession through the sieve of the Gospel so that it could be reclaimed for the sake of terrified consciences. Thus Luther develops five major points in his "A Brief Exhortation to Confession," which is included in the Large Catechism:

> **The focus in Confession and Absolution is not on the confession per se, but on the Absolution.**

First, confession should be voluntary and free of papal tyranny. "No one needs to drive you to confession by commanding it" (LC Confession 20; K-W, 478). Those who do not come to Confession and Absolution out of a sense of their own need can hardly be

---

142  Gerhard Forde, "Absolution: Systematic Considerations," in *The Preached God: Proclamation in Word and Sacrament*, ed. Mark C. Mattes and Steven D. Paulson (Grand Rapids: Eerdmans, 2007), 153.

143  Here note the Apology of the Augsburg Confession: "For we also retain confession especially on account of absolution, which is the Word of God that the power of the keys proclaims to individuals by divine authority. Therefore it would be unconscionable to remove private absolution from the church. Moreover, those who despise private absolution know neither the forgiveness of sins nor the power of the keys" (Ap XII 99–101; K-W, 204).

cajoled by legalistic demands to make a salutary use of this practice. Those who do not come willingly had best stay away: "Hereby we completely abolish the pope's tyranny, commandments, and coercion, for we have no need of them. For, as I have said, we teach this: Let those who do not go to confession willingly and for the sake of absolution just forget about it" (LC Confession 21; K-W, 478). Luther's encouragement is evangelical. Disciples are urged to make use of Confession for the sake of the great treasure that is individually and personally bestowed in the Absolution. Our beggarly neediness, not an ecclesiastical requirement, should incite us to avail ourselves of Confession:

> **Their own consciences would persuade Christians and make them so anxious that they would rejoice and act like poor, miserable beggars who hear that a rich gift of money or clothes is being given out at a certain place; they would hardly need a bailiff to drive and beat them but would run there as fast as they could so as not to miss the gift.**
>
> (LC CONFESSION 23–24; K-W, 478–79)

Second, the practice of confession ought to be free of the unreasonable and tortuous demand that the penitent be able to enumerate their sins. We are absolved for the sake of Christ's merit and on the basis of His divine promise, not on the completeness or comprehensiveness of our own confession. Luther realized that the canonical requirement to enumerate all one's sins led only to a burdened and even more deeply troubled conscience. "We are released from the torture of enumerating all sins in detail" (LC Confession 4; K-W, 476). It is enough to name the sins we know.

Third, people should be taught how to use confession evangelically for the comfort of terrified consciences. Confession is not a good work that we perform but is the occasion to hear Christ's words of pardon and learn how to apply them to our conscience disrupted by guilt and trembling in shame. The goal of confession is not an increase of virtue but of faith in the divine promise.

Fourth, Christian liberty ought not be used as an excuse for setting private Confession aside. Luther complained that some had learned the art of Christian liberty too well: "Unfortunately, people have learned it only too well; they do whatever they please and take advantage of their freedom, acting as if they should or need not go to confession anymore" (LC Confession 5; K-W, 476). Christian freedom is not freedom from the Gospel, and Luther sees the Absolution as purest Gospel. Refusal of the Gospel leaves one not in freedom but in bondage.

Fifth, private Confession stands with other forms of confession in the church. Luther does not separate private or individual Confession from other forms of Confession. We confess our sins daily in the Lord's Prayer: "Indeed, the entire Lord's Prayer is nothing else than such a confession. For what is our prayer but a confession that we neither have nor do what we ought and a plea for grace and a joyful conscience?" (LC Confession 9; K-W, 477). We confess our sins publicly to our neighbors and before God. But in the Large Catechism, Luther is particularly focused on private Confession, which comes into play "when some particular issue weighs on us or attacks us, eating away at us until we can have no peace nor find ourselves sufficiently strong in faith" (LC Confession 13; K-W, 477). For it is here that God has placed His words in a human mouth so that we may hear and know that our sins are forgiven before God in heaven.

These pastoral themes are reflected in Luther's Short Form of Confession, included in the Small Catechism between Holy Baptism and the Sacrament of the Altar. This was intended by Luther to catechize people in the evangelical use of Confession and Absolution. "Luther's discussion of confession, along with the shape of his liturgical rite, shows how he redefines its essence and practice so that it ceases to be a burden and instead becomes an instrument by which the Gospel is conveyed personally to an individual."[144]

In this new version of an ancient rite, the pastor is not there as an ecclesiastical detective to flush out hidden transgressions or as an inspector who must assure that standards of quality control are indiscriminately applied to penitential acts.[145] Neither is the pastor a therapist trafficking in slogans of affirmation, a comforter offering a ministry of presence (whatever that frightening term might mean!), or a coach to get his players enabled for a sanctified life. No, the pastor is here as the ear and the voice of the Good Shepherd. His words of forgiveness are not his own, but those of the Lord who has sent him (see John 20:21–23). These words of Jesus authorize the pastor to speak Christ's own forgiveness in His name and in His stead. Thus Karl-Hermann Kandler writes, "This authorization fundamentally distinguishes confession and absolution from all other forms of therapy; they can surely uncover guilt and failure, but they cannot forgive."[146]

The ear of the pastor becomes the grave that forever conceals the corpse of sin. It is buried there never to be disinterred. In fact, the pastor's ordination vow puts him under orders never to divulge the sins confessed to him. Never means never. Pastors learn to practice God's own forgetfulness of sins (see Psalm 103:9–14). Sins confessed to the pastor are sealed away in silence.

But the pastor's lips are not sealed. He has a verdict to announce on the basis of the death of the Righteous One for the unrighteous. Your sin is now unloaded from your shoulders. It is carried by the Lamb of God, who takes away the sin of the world. He takes it to Calvary. There it was answered for in His own blood.

---

144   Charles Arand, *That I May Be His Own*, 169.

145   Here see Holsten Fagerberg: "Since in confession the pastor appears not as judge but God's voice of forgiveness, he need not investigate the sinner. Absolution covers all sins unconditionally, even those not acknowledged in confession," in *A New Look at the Lutheran Confessions 1529–1537*, trans. Gene J. Lund (St. Louis: Concordia Publishing House, 1972), 223–24. Also see the Apology: "For Christ gave the command to remit sins; ministers administer this command. They do not have a command to investigate secrets. This can be understood from the fact that they remit sins without restriction, sins that not even we ourselves, to whom they are remitted, remember" (Ap XII 105; K-W, 204).

146   Karl-Hermann Kandler, "Luther and the Lutherans on Confession, 'the Forgotten Sacrament,'" *Lutheran Quarterly* 31 (2017): 50–63.

His verdict is the Absolution: "I forgive you all your sins in the name of the Father and of the Son and of the Holy Spirit." That is justification in faith in action. "Therefore, since we have been justified by faith, we have peace with God through our Lord Jesus Christ" (Romans 5:1). In the words of Kandler: "Confession and absolution are thus lived justification."[147]

In the Catechism's Short Form for Confession, Luther notes that the pastor will know additional passages of Scripture to comfort and guide the penitent. Significantly, this comes after the Absolution has been spoken, demonstrating that Christ's forgiveness is now the source of the new life. On the strength of the Absolution, the pastor is able now to counsel the penitent with God's Word so as to guard the conscience and equip the penitent to fight against entanglement in temptation and further enslavement to sin.

# THE OFFICE OF THE KEYS

The section on the Office of the Keys was not composed by Luther himself but added to later editions of the Small Catechism. The Keys belong not to the pope or the clergy but to the Church. It is Christ's holy people who have been endowed with the authority to forgive the sins of all who repent and to bind the sins of those who refuse to repent. The Catechism's teaching is echoed in Luther's *On the Councils and the Church* (1539), where he affirms that "God's people or holy Christians are recognized by the office of the keys exercised publicly" (AE 41:153). Therefore,

> The keys belong not to the pope (as he lies) but to the church, that is, God's people, or to the holy Christian people throughout the entire world, or wherever there are Christians. . . . The keys are the pope's as little as baptism, the sacrament, and the word of God are, for

---

147    Kandler, "Luther and the Lutherans on Confession, 'the Forgotten Sacrament,'" 53.

> they belong to the people of Christ and are called "the church's keys" not "the pope's keys."

> (AE 41:153–54)

Luther's teaching is also confessed in the Treatise on the Power and Primacy of the Pope, where it is "acknowledged that the keys do not belong to one particular person but to the church, as many clear and irrefutable arguments show. For having spoken of the keys in Matthew 18[:18], Christ goes on to say: 'Wherever two or three agree on earth . . .'[Matt. 18:19–20]. Thus, he grants the power of the keys principally and without mediation to the church, and for the same reason the church has primary possession of the right to call ministers" (Tr 24; K-W, 334).

The Keys belong to the whole Church, but they are exercised publicly by those men who are called and ordained into the Office of the Holy Ministry. The authority to forgive and retain sins is given to the Church and is at work, as the Catechism says, "when the called ministers of Christ deal with us by His divine command," that is, forgiving the sins of broken sinners and retaining the sins or those who are secure in their sin. His divine command is given in John 20:22–23. It is carried out in the Church as pastors proclaim the Absolution, whether it be to a solitary individual (as in individual Confession and Absolution) or in a sermon directed to the whole congregation. The Lord wants His disciples to know and trust that through His Word of Absolution their sins are forgiven, and this forgiveness is "as valid and certain, even in heaven, as if Christ our dear Lord dealt with us Himself."

Ministers are not lords over the Church but servants entrusted with the responsibility for proclamation of this Word, which brings forgiveness into the ears and hearts of repentant sinners that they might have life in Jesus now and forever. An old Reformation-era hymn extols the gift:

The words which absolution give
Are His who died that we might live;
The minister whom Christ has sent
Is but His humble instrument.

(*LSB* 614:5)

*FOR FURTHER REFLECTION AND STUDY: CONNECTIONS WITH*
*LUTHER'S SMALL CATECHISM WITH EXPLANATION 2017*

1. Read 2 Samuel 11:1–12:15. How does this narrative demonstrate the dynamic of Confession and Absolution? How was David brought to repentance? How does Nathan respond? (See p. 307.)

2. What are the two parts of Confession? How are they related? (See pp. 307–9.)

3. What does it mean to confess one's sins? (See p. 307.)

4. Why does the Catechism accent the Absolution over the act of Confession? (See pp. 309–11.)

5. If we can confess our sins directly to God, why do we confess them to the pastor? (See pp. 309–311.)

6. Read 1 John 1:8–9. What does God promise here? (See p. 308.)

7. Why is it important that the pastor not in any way violate the confidentiality of Confession? (See p. 310.)

8. Read John 20:23. What is the Absolution? (See p. 310.)

9. How are we to use the Ten Commandments in preparing for Confession? (See p. 311.)

10. Read and mediate on the Penitential Psalms (6; 32; 38; 51; 102; 130; and 143). How do these psalms prepare us for Confession and Absolution? (See p. 311.)

11. If the whole Church possesses the Office of the Keys, why does Christ give His Church pastors? (See pp. 318–20.)

12. What are the biblical qualifications for the pastoral office? (See pp. 320–21.)

# Chapter 7

—⊷∶⊷ ⊷∶⊶—

# The Sacrament of the Altar: Disciples Are Strengthened by Christ's Body and Blood

If now I seek the forgiveness of sins, I do not run to the cross, for I will not find it given there. Nor must I hold to the suffering of Christ, as Dr. Karlstadt trifles, in knowledge or remembrance, for I will not find it there either. But I will find in the sacrament or gospel the word which distributes, presents, offers, and gives to me that forgiveness which was won on the cross.

MARTIN LUTHER, *AGAINST THE HEAVENLY PROPHETS*
(AE 40:214)

The Lord instituted His Supper for His disciples on the night of His betrayal. Matthew, Mark, Luke, and Paul give us their unique accounts, but common to all of them is Jesus' word of promise attached to bread and wine: "This is My body" and "This is My blood." These words set the Lord's Supper apart from the Old Testament Passover and the numerous other meals that Jesus had with His disciples in the days of His earthly ministry.

# What Is the Sacrament of the Altar?

At the original Passover meal, a lamb was roasted and eaten, and its blood was smeared on the doorposts of the houses of Israelites. But in the Lamb of God He Himself establishes, He gives His disciples His body to eat and His blood to drink. The narrative of the Passover has no mention of the forgiveness of sins, but in the Lord's Supper, body and blood are given for the forgiveness of sins. The Lord's Supper is no mere extension or more perfect form of the Passover of the Old Testament; it is its end and fulfillment.

In the meals Jesus shared with disciples in the days of His public ministry, He taught them the purpose of His coming. In the fellowship of a table, He gave Himself intimately and personally to them in conversation. It was at table that Jesus also showed Himself to be the friend of sinners, extending hospitality to lawbreakers and the outcasts of society. But here again, there is no giving of His body to eat and His blood to drink. We do not start with the Passover or with Jesus' meals to understand the Lord's Supper but with the words He uses to establish it.

So Luther answers his own catechetical question "What is the Sacrament of the Altar?" by citing Jesus' words:

> The holy Evangelists Matthew, Mark, Luke, and St. Paul write: Our Lord Jesus Christ, on the night when He was betrayed, took bread, and when He had given thanks, He broke it and gave it to the disciples and said: "Take, eat, this is My body, which is given for you. This do in remembrance of Me." In the same way also He took the cup after supper, and when He had given thanks, He gave it to them, saying, "Drink of it, all of you; this cup is the new testament in My blood, which is shed for you for the forgiveness of sins. This do, as often as you drink it, in remembrance of Me."

With these words, the Lord Jesus does something that is utterly unique. He not only shares a meal with His disciples, but He also establishes for them and all disciples to follow the Supper of the New Testament, His body and blood given for us to eat and to drink. Luther sees these words of Jesus as nothing less than the Gospel itself: "What is the whole gospel but an explanation of this testament?" (AE 35:106).[148]

Disciples are to be taught these words before they are admitted to the Lord's Table: "All this is established from the words Christ used to institute it. So everyone who wishes to be a Christian and to go to the sacrament should know them. For we do not intend to admit to the sacrament and administer it to those who do not know what they seek or why they come" (LC V 1–2; K-W, 467).[149] Without these words of Christ, there is no sacrament. This is why Luther so singularly focuses on them in both of his catechisms.

In a 1528 sermon on the Lord's Supper, Luther reminded the congregation, "Take hold only of the words; they will tell you what the sacrament is" (AE 51:189). Luther answers the question "What is the Sacrament of the Altar?" with an appeal to Christ's Words of Institution. The words of Christ that institute both Baptism and the Lord's Supper bring together command and promise in such a way as the promise "carries out God's mandate," to use the words of Oswald Bayer.[150] Christ's words give what they declare. It is only from the words of the Lord that He used in

**It is only from the words of the Lord that He used in instituting the Lord's Supper that we know what it is and how His words are to be used.**

---

148   Noteworthy is the comment of Sasse: "Luther's explanation of the Words of Institution of the New Testament are an indispensable part of his understanding of the Gospel itself," in "The Formula of Concord's Decision about the Lord's Supper" in *The Lonely Way*, vol. 2, ed. Matthew C. Harrison (St. Louis: Concordia Publishing House, 2002), 39.

149   This statement of Luther lies behind the practice of closed Communion. For more on this, see Matthew C. Harrison and John T. Pless, *Closed Communion? Admission to the Lord's Supper in Biblical Lutheran Perspective* (St. Louis: Concordia Publishing House, 2017).

150   Cited by Peters, *Baptism and Lord's Supper*, 4.

instituting the Lord's Supper that we know what it is and how His words are to be used.[151]

This is a meal with a promise: "given and shed for you for the forgiveness of sins." This meal is no mere memorial to Jesus' atoning death on the cross centuries ago. In this Supper, the Lord delivers the gift of the forgiveness won on the cross with a sure and trustworthy promise that His death for sins was for you. Now under bread and wine, the very body sacrificed on the cross and the very blood that drained from the veins of the Messiah is given to disciples to eat and drink.

Bodily present in the Sacrament, Christ Jesus is extending to us a testament. Luther loves this graphic word, for it clearly indicates that the benefits we are receiving are willed to us by the death of the testator, Jesus Himself. *Testament* entails both incarnation and atonement. If God is to establish a testament, He must die. To die, He takes on our flesh and blood. In his *Babylonian Captivity of the Church* (1520), Luther observes the following:

> For the only difference between a promise and a testament is that the testament involves the death of the one who makes it. A testator is a promiser who is about to die. . . . This testament of Christ is foreshadowed in all the promises of God from the beginning of the world; indeed, whatever value those ancient promises possessed was altogether derived from this new promise that was to come in Christ. Hence the words "compact," "covenant," and "testament of the Lord" occur so frequently in the Scriptures. These words signified that God would one day die. "For where there

---

151    Here also see Luther's comments in his 1523 treatise *The Adoration of the Sacrament*, where he says, "Let go of reason and intellect; for they strive in vain to understand how flesh and blood can be present, and because they do not grasp it they refuse to believe it. Lay hold on the word which Christ speaks: 'Take, this is my body, this is my blood.' One must not do violence to the words of God as to give to any word a meaning other than its natural one, unless there is clear and definite Scripture to do that" (AE 36:279). For more on this point, see Hermann Sasse, *This Is My Body: Luther's Contention for the Real Presence in the Sacrament of the Altar* (Adelaide, South Australia: Lutheran Publishing House, 1977), especially pp. 114–50. An additional comment by Sasse is noteworthy: "Either Jesus meant what he said, or he proposed a puzzle which so far no one has been able to solve" (294–95).

> is a testament, the death of the testator must of neces-
> sity occur" (Heb. 9[:16]). Now God made a testament;
> therefore, it was necessary that he should die. But God
> could not die unless he became man. Thus the incar-
> nation and the death of Christ are both comprehended
> most concisely in this one word, "testament."
>
> (AE 36:38)

The death He dies is one of atonement for the sins of the world. Crucified for our sins and raised from the grave for our justification, He gives us the fruits of His cross, forgiveness of our sins in His body and blood. This testament, Luther says, makes those who receive it in faith heirs of "truly a great, eternal, and unspeakable treasure, namely, the forgiveness of all sins" (AE 35:85).

The Lord gives us His body and blood in, with, and under consecrated bread and wine. Luther dismissed the Roman theory of transubstantiation as a philosophical attempt to explain a biblical mystery. Bread and wine are not transformed in their substance to Christ's body and blood so that these earthly elements cease to exist. Bread and wine remain bread and wine, while at the same time they are the very body and blood of Christ. The Lord's words give what they promise. The bread and wine consecrated by Christ Jesus Himself are His body and blood.

Even as Jesus' words exclude the theory of transubstantiation, so His words may not be twisted to mean that bread and wine represent or signify His body once crucified but now raised from the dead and seated in glory at the Father's right hand but absent from us.[152] Neither are the bread and cup potent symbols that allow us mystically to participate in the life of the crucified and risen Christ. His words say what they mean and mean what they

---

152   Here it is worthwhile to note the words of Reformed theologian Carl Trueman: "Basic to all Reformed under-standings of the Lord's Supper is the idea that it is a sign. This position is shared by those of a more Zwinglian and those of a more Calvinistic persuasion. The choice of bread and wine are not arbitrary but enjoys a connection to what it signifies: the believers' relationship to Christ as articulated through the idea of food and eating," in Robert Kolb and Carl Trueman, *Between Wittenberg and Geneva: Lutheran and Reformed Theology in Conversation* (Grand Rapids: Baker Academic Press, 2017), 197. This volume contains a concise and accurate comparison and contrast of Lutheran and Reformed positions on the Lord's Supper by Kolb and Trueman respectively on pp. 175–205.

say. Jesus gives us His true body and blood to eat and to drink in bread and wine.

The Supper belongs to the Lord. He instituted it in order to give us His body and blood. At this juncture in the Catechism, Luther is echoing words from his 1520 *A Treatise on the New Testament, That Is, the Holy Mass*, where he confessed, "If man is to deal with God and receive anything from him, it must happen in this manner, not that man begins and lays the first stone, but that God alone—without any entreaty or desire of man—must first come and give him a promise" (AE 35:82). The promise that Christ has attached to the bread and wine is that it is His true body and blood given for the forgiveness of our sins. The Lord did not institute His Supper as a sacrifice that His disciples are to perform but as a sacrament to be received, trusting in His gracious words. Hermann Sasse states it well: "The table is called an altar, not because of a sacrifice done there, but because from it what has been sacrificed is given us to be eaten."[153] The Lord's Supper comes as His gift.

> **The Lord did not institute His Supper as a sacrifice that His disciples are to perform but as a sacrament to be received, trusting in His gracious words.**

## What Is the Benefit of This Eating and Drinking?

Having established that the Sacrament is the true body and blood of Christ, Luther then turns to the benefit of this eating and drinking. Eating and drinking do not stand alone as though it were through this act that we gain a spiritual benefit. Bodily eating and drinking are tied to the words of promise: "Given and shed for you for the forgiveness of sins." Luther does not tire of

---

153    Hermann Sasse, "The Lord's Supper in the Catholic Mass," in *The Lonely Way*, vol. 2, 26.

repeating these words, for he is seeking to drive home the point that in Christ's body and blood we are given the forgiveness of sins.[154] Here Christ shows Himself unmistakably to be for you. In the Lord's Supper, Christ delivers the fruits of His redeeming suffering and death. "What is the benefit of such eating and drinking?" is answered: "The words 'given for you' and 'shed for you for the forgiveness of sins' show us that forgiveness of sin, life, and salvation are given to us in the sacrament through these words, because where there is forgiveness of sin, there is also life, and salvation" (SC VI 5–6; K-W, 362). The redemption achieved on the cross is distributed in the body and blood of Christ. In the Sacrament of the Altar, sinners are given to know the consolation of the fact that Christ's forgiveness is for them:

> In the Lord's Supper, Christ delivers the fruits of His redeeming suffering and death.

> Those who go to the sacrament, however, should believe and be assured, not only that they are receiving the true body and blood of Christ in it, but also that it is there given to them and is their own. Why? Not as a work for the sake of money or merit, as the monks and priests hold mass, but for the forgiveness of our sins. Now we surely know what forgiveness of sins means. When he forgives, he forgives everything completely and leaves nothing unforgiven. When I am free of sin, I am also free of death, devil, and hell; I am a son of God, and a lord of heaven and earth. (AE 36:349–50)

---

154  Oswald Bayer rightly concludes, "Luther does not concentrate on the threefold repetition of the two phrases 'given for you' and 'shed for the forgiveness of your sins' just by chance. God's turning toward the sinner, the promise that creates faith empowered by the death and resurrection of Jesus Christ, cannot be summarized any more succinctly and specifically than by using these words. This must be stated clearly as a critique of the depersonalizing speech about the 'bread of life' or the diminution of the Lord's Supper to become a generic lovefest. The Lord's Supper is not some diffuse celebration of life but is defined in a precise way in its essence by means of the connection between the Word of Christ that has effective power and faith," in *Martin Luther's Theology*, 272.

The forgiveness of sins is no mere abstraction, nor is it potentially present. It is there as surely as the bread and wine are the body and blood of Christ given and shed for the world on the cross. Now with His body and blood given into our mouths, Jesus says that it is for you, for the forgiveness of your sins.

In his 1525 treatise *Against the Heavenly Prophets*, Luther asserted:

> If now I seek the forgiveness of sins, I do not run to the cross, for I will not find it given there. Nor must I hold to the suffering of Christ, as Dr. Karlstadt trifles, in knowledge or remembrance, for I will not find it there either. But I will find in the sacrament or gospel the word which distributes, presents, offers, and gives to me that forgiveness which was won on the cross.
>
> (AE 40: 214)

This theme lies behind the Small Catechism's question on the benefit of eating and drinking in the Sacrament. It is also echoed in the Large Catechism, where Luther confesses the historical reality of Christ's death on the cross for sin and the distribution of this treasure by way of Christ's promise:

> Although the work took place on the cross and forgiveness of sins has been acquired, yet it cannot come to us in any other way than through the Word. How should we know that this took place or was to be given to us if it were not proclaimed by preaching, by the oral Word? From what source do they know of forgiveness, and how can they grasp and appropriate it, except by steadfastly believing the Scriptures and the gospel?
>
> (LC V 31; K-W, 469–70)

Luther sees in the Lord's Supper the most concentrated form of the Gospel[155] because in it the death of Christ is proclaimed

---

155 Also note Peters: "For him [Luther], the Lord's Supper is not an offering and a good work performed by a human

and the benefits of that saving death are bestowed in His body and blood given us to eat and drink. Satan may attack as he wills. Your own flesh may be weak and weary in the struggle against sin. Death may threaten your life. Nevertheless, with His body and blood Christ declares Himself to be for you. Luther directs disciples to the consoling nature of the Lord's Supper:

> The devil is a furious enemy; . . . when he cannot rout us by force, he sneaks and skulks about at every turn, trying all kinds of tricks, and does not stop until he has finally worn us out so that we either renounce our faith or lose heart and become indifferent or impatient. For times like these, when our heart feels too sorely pressed, this comfort of the Lord's Supper is given to bring us new strength and refreshment.

**With His body and blood Christ declares Himself to be for you.**

(LC V 26–27, K-W, 469)

This is why disciples treasure the Sacrament of the Altar; it gives us the very body and blood of our crucified and risen Savior as the certain and sure pledge that He will not abandon us in our despair or forsake us in death.

## HOW CAN BODILY EATING AND DRINKING DO SUCH GREAT THINGS?

Risen from the dead, the Lord Jesus comes to His disciples with His body and blood in the Sacrament. In this way, He is fulfilling the promise of Matthew 28:20 to be with us always, even to the end of the age. The observation of Werner Elert is helpful here: "We can neither baptize nor celebrate the Holy

---

being in Christ before God; it is a testament and sacrament of God through Christ for us. As such it is the *summa et compendium Euangelii,*" in *Baptism and Lord's Supper,* 21.

Communion as though Christ had not risen. By the same token we can also understand the promises attached to the sacraments only if they are linked to Him who overcame death."[156] In the Lord's Supper, it is the Lord's death that is proclaimed in the eating and drinking as the apostle states in 1 Corinthians 10:16: "The cup of blessing that we bless, is it not a participation in the blood of Christ? The bread that we break, is it not a participation in the body of Christ?" The Lord's Supper would not be what it is—the body and blood of Christ given us to eat and drink—without the atoning death of Jesus on the cross. If the Lord had died but not been raised from the dead, the Sacrament of the Altar would be empty, nothing more than a memorial meal for a dead man. Raised from the dead, Jesus lives to give us life. The life He gives is in His body and blood.

## WHO RECEIVES THIS SACRAMENT WORTHILY?

Christ's body and blood are given in the Lord's Supper even to those who come to the altar without faith, but it is only through faith that the benefits of Christ are received. "Whoever believes these very words [given for you and shed for you for the forgiveness of sins] has what they declare and state, namely, 'forgiveness of sins'" (SC V 8; K-W, 362). The mouth eats and drinks, while the heart lays hold of the promise attached to Christ's body and blood, given and shed for you. Peters writes:

> Both the external human being's body and the inner person of the heart are connected directly with Christ's body that was offered and the blood of the covenant. The Lord draws near to the external, physical man

---

156    Werner Elert, *The Lord's Supper Today*, trans. Martin Bertram and Rudolph F. Norden (St. Louis: Concordia Publishing House, 1973),10.

under the gifts of creation and the inner man under
the promise of grace.[157]

In the Catechism, Luther coordinates the physical eating and
drinking with faith in Christ's testamentary words.

Luther addresses the use of the Lord's Supper under the question "Who, then, receives this sacrament worthily?" Robert Kolb
observes, "In this question the affirmation of the impact of the
Lord's Supper on those who receive it only through trust in the
promise places the Supper squarely in the middle of daily life."[158]
Luther's focus is on Christ's words of promise and the faith that
sticks with those words in the midst of the uncertainty brought
about by establishing worthiness to receive the Lord's Supper of
humanly established standards, such as fasting or other exercises
of piety.

In his Catechism sermon from 1528 on the Lord's Supper, Luther
uses language that will also show up in the Large Catechism, that
the Lord's Supper is "not a poison but an antidote, which means
salvation" (AE 51:192).[159] Pastorally, Luther aims to encourage a
salutary partaking of the Lord's body and blood that avoids undue
fear on the one hand and laxity on the other hand. Fasting and
the like are external disciplines that have their usefulness in so far
as they go, but as Luther says the person who has faith in Christ's
words "is truly worthy and well prepared" because the promise
of the forgiveness of sins "can be received in no other way than

---

157   Peters, *Baptism and Lord's Supper*, 196.

158   Robert Kolb, "The Lord's Supper in the Lutheran Tradition," in *Between Wittenberg and Geneva*, 177.

159   Compare with the Large Catechism: "Why, then, do we act as if the sacrament were a poison that would kill
us if we ate of it?" (LC V 68; K-W, 474).

by faith" (LC V 34; K-W, 470).[160] This thought is expressed in Luther's reworking of a hymn on the Lord's Supper by John Huss:[161]

> Jesus here Himself is sharing;
> Heed then how you are preparing,
> For if you do not believe,
> His judgment then you shall receive.
>
> (*LSB* 627:3; © 1980 and 2006 CPH)

But the right preparation for eating and drinking the Lord's body and blood is not a work that makes one worthy of the Sacrament; it is faith in the words and promises of Jesus. So stanzas 5–9 provide clarity as to how disciples prepare for the Lord's Supper:

> Firmly hold with faith unshaken
> That this food is to be taken
> By the sick who are distressed,
> By hearts that long for peace and rest.
>
> Agony and bitter labor
> Were the cost of God's high favor;
> Do not come if you suppose
> You need not need Him who died and rose.
>
> Christ says: "Come, all you that labor,
> And receive My grace and favor:
> Those who feel no pain or ill
> Need no physician's help or skill.

---

160    Also see Luther's continuation of this thought a few lines later: "Now this is the sum total of a Christian's preparation to receive this sacrament worthily. Because this treasure is fully offered in the words, it can be grasped and appropriated only by the heart. Such a gift and eternal treasure cannot be seized with the hand. Fasting, prayer, and the like may have their place as an external preparation and children's exercise so that one's body may behave properly and reverently toward the body and blood of Christ. But the body cannot grasp and appropriate what is given in and with the sacrament. This is done by the faith of the heart that discerns and desires such a treasure" (LC V 36–37; K-W, 470). Faith does nor bodily eating and drinking do not constitute the sacrament but it is only by faith in Christ's words that one receives the benefits of the sacrament in the eating and drinking of Christ's body and blood.

161    Robin Leaver notes that Luther's thoroughgoing renovation of the hymn by Huss demonstrates that Luther uses it to elucidate the confession of the Sacrament of the Altar. "The hymn *Jesus Christus unser Heiland* of 1524 therefore contains echoes in substance and in content of his various treatises on the Sacrament of the Altar written in the previous years, demonstrating an underlying consistence of thinking," in *Luther's Liturgical Music: Principles and Implications* (Grand Rapids: Eerdmans, 2007), 157. Leaver provides an excellent textual study of this catechetical hymn, 153–60.

"For what purpose was My dying
If not for your justifying?
And what use this precious food
If you yourself were pure and good?"

If your heart this truth professes
And your mouth your sin confesses,
You will be your Savior's guest,
Be at His banquet truly blest.

(*LSB* 627:5–9; sts. 6, 8 © 1980 and 2006 CPH)

Disciples will come often to the Lord's Supper, for they hunger and thirst for what their Lord gives with His body and blood: the strengthening of their faith in the forgiveness of their sins, the food that nourishes our life with God here in time, and the pledge of the resurrection of our bodies to life everlasting. Our need and Christ's promises compel us to seek the Sacrament often. The Lord's Supper is our food along the way, even as it also is Christ's own guarantee that death will not have the final word. Erich Schick, a pastoral theologian of the last century, put it nicely: "Let us go to the Table of the Lord as if we were going to meet death so that one day we may go to meet death as if we were going to the Table of the Lord."[162]

> **Disciples will come often to the Lord's Supper, for they hunger and thirst for what their Lord gives.**

Enlivened by the gift of Jesus' testament, disciples now return to the world, alive by faith in Christ's promises and living in love toward the neighbor. This is expressed in the Post-Communion Collect that Luther added to the liturgy in 1526, in which we give thanks for the salutary gift of Jesus' body and blood and implore the Father that it would strengthen us in faith toward Him and in fervent love for one another. It is also given doxological expression in the last stanza of the above-mentioned hymn:

---

162    Erich Schick, "Altar Stairs," in *The Minister's Prayer Book* (Philadelphia: Muhlenberg Press, 1986), 381.

> Let this food your faith so nourish
> That its fruit of love may flourish
> And your neighbor learn from you
> How much God's wondrous love can do.
>
> (*LSB* 627:10; © 1980 and 2006 CPH)

Receiving the fruits of Christ's once and for all sacrifice on the cross in the Sacrament, disciples are turned outward to live sacrificially for the benefit and blessing of their neighbors in this world. Mercy received in Christ's body and blood is then mercy given to those who live in need and suffering in a fallen creation. Luther captures this connection in his 1526 treatise *The Sacrament of the Body and Blood of Christ: Against the Fanatics*:

> For it is necessary for each one to know that Christ has given his body, flesh, and blood on the cross to be our treasure and to help us to receive forgiveness of sins, that is, that we may be saved, redeemed from death and hell. That is the first principle of Christian doctrine. It is presented to us in the words, and his body and blood are given to us to be received corporeally as a token and confirmation of this fact. To be sure, he did this only once, carrying it out and achieving it on the cross; but he causes it each day anew to be set before us, distributed and poured out through preaching, and he orders us to remember him always and never forget him. The second principle is love. It is demonstrated in the first place by the fact that he has left us an example. *As he gives himself for us with his body and blood in order to redeem us from all misery, so we too are to give ourselves with might and main for our neighbor.*
>
> (AE 36:352, EMPHASIS ADDED)

Luther does not see the Lord's Supper as an end in and of itself. It was instituted by Christ to strengthen our faith in His blood-bought forgiveness of sins and in that forgiveness give us life and salvation. These are gifts that bind us together in Christ with one another.

## For Further Reflection and Study: Connections with Luther's Small Catechism with Explanation 2017

1.  What is the significance of Jesus' "timing" ("on the night when He was betrayed") for the instituting of the Sacrament of the Altar? Read Matthew 26:17–30. (See p. 323.)

2.  What is the pledge that Jesus gives us in this Sacrament? (See p. 323.)

3.  How are we to understand the presence of Christ's body and blood in the Sacrament? (See pp. 324–25.)

4.  Read Hebrews 9:11–22. What is required for a testament? How is the Lord's Supper a "new testament"? (See pp. 324–25.)

5.  Read Exodus 24:1–11. What happens with the blood? What does the blood of Christ do for us in the Lord's Supper? (See p. 325.)

6.  Read 1 Corinthians 10:16. Where do we participate in the body and blood of Christ? (See p. 325.)

7.  Read Hebrews 10:12–14. Jesus' death is the once and for all sacrifice for sin. Therefore, the Lord's Supper is not a sacrifice that we offer to God. How do Jesus' words make it clear that in the Lord's Supper we are receiving the fruits of His sacrifice? (See pp. 327–28.)

8.  The pastor speaks the words of Jesus (Words of Institution) over the bread and wine. What do these words do? (See p. 328.)

9.  What is "transubstantiation"? How does Scripture speak against this view (see 1 Corinthians 11:26)? (See p. 329.)

10. How do the words of Christ challenge the teaching of many Protestants that the bread and wine are signs, or symbols, for the body and blood of Christ? (See pp. 329–30.)

11. Review Luther's explanation of the Second Article of the Creed. There Luther confesses that by His death Christ redeemed us "from all sins, from death, and from the power of the devil." How are these benefits, obtained by Christ on the cross, now delivered to us in the Sacrament? (See pp. 331–33.)

12. Read Leviticus 17:10–14. In this passage, God strictly forbids the eating of blood. But in the Lord's Supper, the same Lord instructs us to drink His blood. What promises are attached to Christ's blood? See 1 Peter 1:18–19 and Hebrews 9:11–14, 22. (See p. 332.)

13. Why should disciples of Jesus receive the Lord's Supper frequently? (See pp. 333–34.)

14. Eating and drinking are bodily functions. How do they provide spiritual benefits? (See pp. 335–36.)

15. Is the forgiveness of sins automatic for all who eat and drink Jesus' body and blood? (See pp. 336–37.)

16. How can I best prepare to receive the Lord's Supper worthily? (See pp. 338–41.)

17. Should Christians with a weak faith come to the Sacrament? (See p. 341.)

18. What do we "share with others" who come to the Lord's Supper with us? How does this help us understand "closed Communion"? (See pp. 343–44.)

*Chapter 8*

———✦·✦·✦·✦———

# Daily Prayers: Disciples Thank and Praise the Holy Trinity

Evening and morning,
Sunset and dawning,
   Wealth, peace, and gladness
   Comfort in sadness:
These are Thy works; all the glory be Thine!
Times without number,
Awake or in slumber,
   Thine eye observes us,
   From danger preserves us,
Causing Thy mercy upon us to shine.

PAUL GERHARDT
(*LSB* 726:1)

The disciple is given to "pray without ceasing, give thanks in all circumstances; for this is the will of God in Christ Jesus for you" (1 Thessalonians 5:17–18). Luther begins his celebrated letter to Peter, his barber, "A Simple Way to Pray," echoing a saying attributed to Jerome, "Everything a believer does is prayer," noting that daily work is transformed into prayer when it is carried out by those who fear and honor God.[163] Nevertheless, Luther reminds the village barber that having set times and practices for daily prayer is a salutary thing. "It is a good thing to let

---

163   Martin Luther, "A Simple Way to Pray," In *Pastoral Writings*, vol. 4 of *The Annotated Luther*, ed. Mary Jane Haemig (Minneapolis: Fortress Press, 2016), 257.

prayer be the first business of the morning and the last at night."[164] Drawing on Psalm 1 with its description of the blessed man who mediates on the Word of the Lord day and night, Luther urges his readers to attend to a discipline of genuine prayer: "Yet we must be careful not to break the habit of true prayer and imagine other works to be necessary which, after all, are nothing of the kind. Thus at the end we become lazy and lax, cold and listless toward prayer."[165]

Luther's Catechism itself provided such a discipline for the life of prayer as he specified a simple but concrete pattern for daily prayer in the morning and evening and at mealtime. The day's beginning and ending are particularly appropriate for prayers of thanksgiving and supplication, as God is recognized as the One who is responsible for our life and being. Mealtimes, too, evoke prayers of thanksgiving for the gift of daily bread. In a very real sense, the daily prayers appended to the Catechism demonstrate that the Catechism not only teaches us about prayer but is also itself a tool for prayer as, within the daily rhythms of creaturely life, we look to God for every good thing, entrust our fragile lives into His merciful keeping, and acknowledge His benefits with thanksgiving. Since Luther understood prayer as the "Christian's true office and function" (AE 24:87), it is not surprising that he includes these helps for the daily prayer life of the disciple to help develop this discipline.

> **The Catechism not only teaches us about prayer but is itself a tool for prayer as within the daily rhythms of creaturely life.**

C. F. W. Walther reflected Luther's teaching on prayer when he wrote that "prayer is neither a meritorious act, nor a Means of Grace, rather an exercise of faith on the part of the one redeemed."[166] In praying the Catechism, faith is exercised as the disciple calls

---

164    Luther, "A Simple Way to Pray," 257.

165    Luther, "A Simple Way to Pray," 258.

166    C. F. W. Walther, "Prayer," in *All Glory to God* (St. Louis: Concordia Publishing House, 2016), 404.

on the Lord according to His command and promise, holding fast to Christ in suffering and in joy. We might say that Luther has structured the first three parts of the Catechism in such a way as to lead to prayer: Command (Decalogue), Promise (Apostles' Creed), and Prayer (the Lord's Prayer). Now at the end of the Catechism, Luther provides some specific suggestions for ways in which faith is exercised in daily prayer.

## MORNING PRAYER AND EVENING PRAYER

Luther's Morning and Evening Prayers share a common template:

- **Blessing in the name of the triune God with the sign of the holy cross**

- **Confession of the Apostles' Creed**

- **Praying the Lord's Prayer**

- **Morning/Evening Prayer**

- **"Then go joyfully to your work . . ."/"Then go to sleep at once . . ."**

By beginning and ending the day in the name of the triune God, Luther is locating the life of the disciple under the work of the Father, Son, and Holy Spirit. This is helpfully described by Carl Beckwith:

> The same sign of the cross and the same confession of the Trinity made upon you at your baptism is acted out and spoken again by you as you rise to start your day and as you retire at the end of your day. By framing the Christian life this way, Luther places before the believer the daily remembrance of baptism and its benefits, and furthermore construes daily living according to the saving work of the Trinity. This is

not a mere remembrance but daily participation in the saving event of baptism. Both aspects of the believer are united in the Trinitarian confession of baptism and baptismal living. . . . For Luther, Christian salvation, identity, and ethics find their coherence and grammar in the Trinity and our trinitarian confession. We live in Christ by the Holy Spirit to the delight of the Father.[167]

This is given doxological expression in Johann Jacob Rambach's hymn:

> Baptized into Your name most holy,
> O Father, Son, and Holy Ghost,
> I claim a place though weak and lowly,
> Among Your saints, Your chosen host.
> Buried with Christ and dead to sin,
> Your Spirit now shall live within.
>
> (*LSB* 590:1)

Beginning and concluding the day by calling on the Lord's name given in Baptism, disciples see their lives from the perspective of the Father, who has willed our salvation accomplished in the Son and delivered by the Holy Spirit. The course of daily life, including its uncertainties, is lived within the promising word and work of the triune God. Disciples need not fear dangers in the day or during the night, for their lives are kept secure in the Lord's name. The disciple, awake or asleep, has this comfort: "I am baptized, instructed with the Word alone, absolved, and partake of the Lord's Supper. But with the Word and through the Word, the Holy Spirit is present, and the whole Trinity works salvation, as the words of Baptism declare" (AE 8:264).[168]

---

167 Carl Beckwith, *Confessional Lutheran Dogmatics*, vol. 3, 5. Also note Edmund Schlink's comment: "Luther's direction to the head of the family as to how he should teach the members of his household to bless themselves in the name of the triune God by saying, 'In the name of God, the Father, the Son, and the Holy Spirit. Amen' is not a dead relic of antiquated doctrine nor a fossilized custom," in *Theology of the Lutheran Confessions*, 65.

168 Note here how Luther's thought parallels the morning hymn by the sixteenth-century hymnist Martin Behm, "O Blessed, Holy Trinity" (*LSB* 876).

The Apostles' Creed is an exposition of the triune name of God. First confessed over the disciple in Holy Baptism, it now brackets the day in faith. The Apostles' Creed functions in four dimensions in Morning and Evening Prayer. First, it is a recital of the work of God in the disciple's creation, redemption, and sanctification. Luther "personalizes" his explanation of each of the three articles so that the one who is confessing the Creed is recognizing himself or herself as the one who is receiving gifts from the God who is Father, Son, and Holy Spirit. "He has made me . . . He has redeemed me, a lost and condemned person.

> **The one who is confessing the Creed is recognizing himself or herself as the one who is receiving gifts from the God who is Father, Son, and Holy Spirit.**

. . . He has called me by the Gospel." In this way, Luther uses the Creed, which in turn will leave its imprint on his two short prayers for morning and evening.

Second, the Creed is the response of faith. In the Prologue of the First Commandment, God identifies Himself as our God: "I am the LORD your God" (Exodus 20:1). As Luther sees the Creed as an answer to the First Commandment, we now say back to God what He has first said to us. He is the Father who created me in body and soul. He is the Lord who has purchased and won me by His blood. He is the Holy Spirit who has called me to faith. The Creed is the faith once delivered to the saints, that is, the content of the apostles' doctrine (Acts 2:42) given us in Holy Scripture, which we now claim as ours by faith as we trust God's Word.

Third, the Creed is a renunciation of Satan. Just as in Holy Baptism, disciples renounce the devil with all his works and ways, so each day as we begin and end the day, we are saying "No" to the evil one and his empty deceit. The Creed confesses the faith that is "the shield of faith" (see Ephesians 6:16) that extinguishes the flaming darts of the devil, who seeks our destruction.

Luther's short prayers draw this out as we pray in light of Psalm 91, "Let Your holy angel be with me, that the evil foe may have no power over me."

Fourth, the Creed is doxology. It is a joyful and glad confession of praise to the triune God for who He is, and it evokes thanksgiving for the bounty of His gifts in each of the three articles.[169] In this way, the Creed also is foundational for the thanksgiving contained in Luther's Morning and Evening Prayers.

The Lord's Prayer follows the Creed, as the faith that is confessed is now prayed. The Spirit endows with boldness, and the Son supplies us with confidence to address God as our Father. It is only through the faith we have confessed with lips and believe in the heart that we are enabled to pray as dear children address a dear father. The expansiveness of the Lord's Prayer does indeed span the world, bringing all that we need in body and soul before God the Father Almighty at the day's beginning and at its end. The life of discipleship is lived to and from this prayer. It is fitting that it is prayed as we rise from sleep and as we sink back into nocturnal rest. The Father who tenderly invites us to pray this way is the Father Almighty, the Maker of heaven and earth who neither sleeps nor slumbers. He is the Creator who preserves our going out and coming in (Psalm 121).

> **The expansiveness of the Lord's Prayer does indeed span the world, bringing all that we need in body and soul before God, the Father Almighty.**

Crafted by Luther out of the Church's long tradition of morning and evening prayers, his terse and easily memorable catechetical prayers flow out of the Creed and the Lord's Prayer. Both prayers open with thanksgiving and conclude with a petition that God would deliver us from the cunning assaults of the old evil foe. In the

---

169 What Holsten Fagerberg says of the First Article may be expanded to include the Second and Third Articles as well: "God richly provides us with His gifts day by day. The First Article is a grateful song of praise to the Giver of many good gifts," in *A New Look at the Lutheran Confessions (1529–1537)*, 117. This doxological use of the Creed is also reflected in Luther's hymn "We All Believe in One True God" (*LSB* 954).

morning, we render thanks to our heavenly Father through His Son that He has kept us from all harm and danger, recalling the language of Luther's explanation of the First Article, where he states that God "defends me against all danger and guards and protects me from all evil." In the evening, the formula of thanksgiving to the Father through the Son is repeated as acknowledgment that He has "graciously kept me this day."

In the Morning Prayer is the petition that God "would keep me this day also from sin and every evil, that all my doings and life may please You." Here the disciple implores the Father for protection from the perils that are ever-present in this fallen creation, including acts of unbelief that arise from a polluted heart and corruption that threatens to distort the life God has given. Driven by impulses of the flesh from within and surrounded by chaotic forces from without, we "walk in danger all the way," to use the words of an old hymn (*LSB* 716:1). Without God's fatherly intervention, we are exposed to forces that are too powerful for us. Left to itself, the heart strays, and we wonder haplessly into sin and embrace the evil rather than the good that God intends for His people. In Luther's little prayer, we find an echo of the ancient Te Deum, "Grant, O Lord, to keep us this day without sin" (*LSB*, p. 225).

At the day's close is the supplication for God's forgiveness for where we have failed: "I pray that You would forgive me all my sins where I have done wrong." It is only under the blanket of God's merciful absolution that we can lie down and sleep in peace (Psalm 4:8), and so we implore God that He would "graciously keep me this night." The Lord's forgiveness expels worry and excommunicates anxiety so that we can sleep in peace. Confident in God's merciful providence, we disciples of Jesus Christ may sleep in the knowledge that we are secure for time and eternity in His keeping.

Both prayers culminate with a commendation and recapitulation of the Seventh Petition: "For into Your hands I commend myself, my body and soul, and all things. Let Your holy angel be with me, that the evil foe may have no power over me." Here Luther echoes Psalms 31:5, 8, 15 and 91:9–11.

The structure of both prayers can be diagramed as follows[170]:

| MORNING | EVENING |
|---|---|
| I thank You, my heavenly Father, through Jesus Christ, Your dear Son, ||
| that You have kept me this night from all harm and danger; | that You have graciously kept me this day; |
| and I pray that ||
| You would keep me this day also from sin and every evil, that all my doings and life may please You. | You would forgive me all my sins where I have done wrong, and graciously keep me this night. |

For into Your hands I commend myself, my body and soul, and all things. Let Your holy angel be with me, that the evil foe may have no power over me. Amen.

The rubric at the conclusion of Morning Prayer directs disciples toward their callings in the world: "Then go joyfully to your work, singing a hymn, like that of the Ten Commandments, or whatever your devotion may suggest." The life of prayer does not displace daily work and responsibilities, but instead these tasks are taken up in the confidence that God's commandments direct us to God-pleasing service of the neighbor. Good works are not self-chosen but are

> **The life of prayer does not displace daily work and responsibilities, but instead these tasks are taken up in the confidence that God's commandments direct us to God-pleasing service of the neighbor.**

---

170   This diagram is based on the description by Albrecht Peters in *Commentary on Luther's Catechisms: Confession and the Christian Life*, trans. Thomas H. Trapp (St. Louis: Concordia Publishing House, 2013), 236.

identified by the Ten Commandments, which show us His will for the life of the redeemed in this old creation.

Likewise, Luther supplies a simple directive at the end of the Evening Prayer: "Then go to sleep at once and in good cheer." There is no need to lie awake in fear and uncertainty, for Christ Jesus has made me His own. God is praised when His disciples get a good night's sleep. The Lord gives to His beloved children sleep, and so it is received with faith in His promises (see Psalm 127:2).

Time for both work and rest are received by the Lord's disciples with thanksgiving. Both come from the Lord God and are so recognized by prayers before going to work[171] and returning to rest.

## ASKING A BLESSING AND RETURNING THANKS

Mealtime is also an occasion for blessing God and receiving our daily bread with thanksgiving. In the Garden of Eden, God gave Adam food to satisfy his hunger (see Genesis 1:30; 2:16). After the fall into sin, food did not come to our first parents easily or without a struggle to plant and harvest (see Genesis 3:17–19), yet God in His mercy continued to provide seedtime and harvest (Genesis 8:22), adding meat to the human menu (Genesis 9:3). God is blessed as the donor of every good thing, including food and drink, and so it is received with reverence, acknowledging that these mundane and necessary fruits of the earth are holy (see 1 Timothy 4:4–5). For this reason, Luther prefaces his "table liturgy" with this rubric: "The children and members of the household shall go to the table reverently, fold their hands."

Then something like an introit comes from Psalm 145:15–16, as God is acknowledged as the Creator and benefactor to whom the

---

171 Here note the comment of Hans Walter Wolff: "The time of man is above all time conferred on him. His work is useless and meaningless when he forgets this. The Old Testament wisdom indeed plainly calls man from laziness; but it warns in still strong terms against the misunderstanding that man receives the gifts he has only through his own work," in *Anthropology of the Old Testament*, 134.

eyes of all look as He gives "them their food at the proper time," opening His "hand [to] satisfy the desires of every living thing." Psalm 145, like other psalms of thanksgiving (see, for example, Psalm 104), acclaims the Lord God as the One who provides for all that is necessary for life to flourish.

The Lord's Prayer is prayed, for in it we are taught to say, "Give us this day our daily bread." With a prayer of blessing, disciples recognize where food and drink come from. These are not mere commodities that we acquire for ourselves by our labor, creativity, strength, or cleverness. Food and drink are gifts from the Father's bountiful goodness and are received as such through Jesus Christ, our Lord.

*For Further Reflection and Study: Connections with*
*Luther's Small Catechism with Explanation 2017*

1. Why did Luther provide prayers for morning, evening, and mealtime? (See p. 346.)

2. Why do the Morning and Evening Prayers begin with blessing in the name of the triune God? (See pp. 346–47.)

3. What is the purpose of making the sign of the cross? (See p. 347.)

4. What are the four functions of the Apostles' Creed in daily prayer? (See p. 347.)

5. How does the Creed form a foundation for our praying the Lord's Prayer as Jesus intends us to pray it? (See p. 347.)

6. Look up Psalms 31:5 and 91:11. How do you see these verses reflected in Luther's Morning Prayer? (See p. 347.)

7. Study Luther's catechism hymn on the Ten Commandments, "These Are the Holy Ten Commands" (*LSB* 581). How does this hymn focus the commandments toward our daily life and work? Why do you think Luther suggested it for use in morning devotions?

8. How is Luther's Evening Prayer like his Morning Prayer? How is it different? (See pp. 346–47.)

9. Read Psalms 4:8; 121; 127. How are these reflected in Luther's Evening Prayer? (See p. 347.)

10. Study the hymn "I Lie, O Lord, within Your Care" (*LSB* 885). How might it help you fulfill Luther's directive "Then go to sleep at once and in good cheer"?

11. How do Luther's mealtime prayers flow from his explanation of the Fourth Petition? (See pp. 347–48.)

12. Read Psalm 145:15–16. Where does it focus our attention as we prepare to eat? (See p. 348.)

13. Read Psalms 136:1, 25; 147:9–11. How do these texts shape our giving of thanks? (See p. 348.)

14. Read Psalm 103:2. What are the Lord's benefits? How are we to respond to them? (See p. 348.)

15. Read 1 Timothy 4:4–5. What does this passage teach us about God's gifts of the First Article and daily bread? (See p. 348.)

# Chapter 9

———— ✦ ·✦· ✦ ————

# Table of Duties: Disciples in the World

Reason is the devil's bride, which plans some particular course because it does not know what may please God. . . . The best and highest station in life is to love God and one's neighbor. Indeed that station is filled by the ordinary manservant or maidservant who cleans the meanest pot.

CITED FROM
*LUTHER'S EXPOSITION OF THE SERMON ON THE MOUNT*
BY GUSTAF WINGREN, *LUTHER ON VOCATION*, 88

D isciples are not called out of the world but are called to live in creation, with faithfulness to their Lord and in loving service to the neighbor. It is within the ordinary places of life that God is to be served and obeyed. The Table of Duties stands against the backdrop of the First Article, the Fourth Petition, and the second table of the Decalogue. The Father who has made me and all creatures sets my life in the network of relationships to other human beings in what Luther called the three estates of church, civil community, and household.

Lying behind Luther's treatment of the Table of Duties is his understanding of the "three estates." Sometimes referred to as the

> ———— ✦ ·✦· ✦ ————
>
> **The Father who has made me and all creatures sets my life in the network of relationships to other human beings.**
>
> ———— ✦ ·✦· ✦ ————

three hierarchies, or orders, of church, household, and state, this triad is found in the medieval tradition as a way of delineating stations or structures of life that human beings occupy within an ordered community. In this ordered community, human beings have the responsibility to discharge particular social duties. This tripartite ordering was characteristic of medieval interpretations of Aristotelian ethics. Luther used these categories in confessing God's creative work in establishing the places where human life is preserved. The three estates are instituted by God and are upheld by His Word for the curbing of the effects of sin and the flourishing of humanity. In contrast to the monastic notion of the superior form of the spiritual life as an ascetic withdrawal from the earthly and temporal, Luther understood the place of the Christian life to be in the world in these "three fundamental forms of life."[172] In his lecture on Psalm 111 (1530), Luther said "these divine stations continue and remain throughout all kingdoms, as wide as the world and to the end of the world" (AE 13:369). Luther also wrote of the three estates in his 1539 *On the Councils and the Church*, where he identified these three hierarchies as "ordained by God," saying that "we need no more; indeed, we have enough and more than enough to do in living aright and resisting the devil in these three" (AE 41:177). Here the Reformer used these three God-ordained estates as a polemic against the self-chosen works of religious orders.

The most succinct treatment of the estates in Luther is his summary of the teaching in the *Confession Concerning Christ's Supper* (1528). Here he declared that "the holy orders and true religious institutions established by God are these three: the office of the priest, the estate of marriage, the civil government" (AE 37:364). Faith is not bound to any particular order or estate and is found in all three estates, but none of them are paths to righteousness

---

172    Bayer, *Martin Luther's Theology*, 122. Also see Bayer's essays "Nature and Institution: *Luther's Doctrine of the Three Estates*" (90–118) and "Luther's Ethics as Pastoral Care" (119–37) in *Freedom in Response*. Bayer makes the argument that Luther's ethic was one of radical obedience to the First Commandment lived out, not by abandonment of the world but within the three estates instituted by God.

before God; instead, they are the concrete locations where faith is active in love for the well-being of the neighbor.

> **Above these three institutions and orders is the common order of Christian love, in which one serves not only the three orders, but also serves every needy person in general with all kinds of benevolent deeds, such as feeding the hungry, giving drink to the thirsty, forgiving enemies, praying for all men on earth, suffering all kinds of evil on earth, etc. Behold, all of these are called good and holy works. However, none of these orders is a means of salvation. There remains only one way above them all, viz. faith in Jesus Christ.**
>
> (AE 37:365)

These estates were for Luther "holy orders," for they were sanctified by God's Word. Every human being, according to Luther, lives in all three estates because everyone is bound by obligations to God and the neighbor. It is the Christian who by faith recognizes that these estates are created by God and are works of His providential care for the good of His creation. In Luther's view, God is hidden behind the masks of those who fill various stations in the estates, using them as instruments for his ongoing work on behalf of human beings.

The first estate established in creation is the church, the place of God's speaking and human beings answering. Just as the First Commandment is fundamental and universal, so human beings are created to worship their Creator and cannot escape this demand, even when the response is unbelief. In his Genesis lectures, Luther spoke of the establishment of a church "without walls" (AE 1:103) preceding both the household and state. After the fall, the church as an order of creation remains, but it is corrupted by unbelief, which is false worship. Rather than clinging to the promise of grace and blessing, human beings exchange the truth of God for a lie and worship the creature instead of the Creator (see Romans 1:25).

Household, the second estate, is inclusive not only of the nuclear family but also of all those who live and work under the same roof. Marriage is at the center of this estate, for through this union God creates and nurtures new human life. This is the place where daily bread is given and received. Living before the industrial revolution, where daily work was generally separated from the home, Luther saw work in the context of the family and for the good of these people who are the nearest neighbors.

If the second estate produces life, the third estate protects, guards, and defends life. The third estate, the political order, was founded on the household for the Reformer, as "all other authority is derived and developed out of the authority of parents" (LC I:141; K-W, 405). After the fall, there is a necessity to this estate in Luther's thinking, for it functions as a coercive means to prevent human society from collapsing into complete chaos and corruption: "There was no government of the state before sin, for there was no need of it. Civil government is a remedy required by our corrupted nature. It is necessary that lust be held in check by the bonds of the laws and by penalties" (AE 1:104). Government, according to Luther, was established in creation out of the household, but the state was established after the fall.

The three estates were articulated in the Small Catechism as the Table of Duties (*Die Haustafel* or "The Household Chart of Some Bible Passages"), where Luther provides a catalog of biblical texts "for various holy orders" modeled after Jean Gerson's *Tractate Concerning the Way of Life for All the Faithful.* Here Luther makes use of the term "holy orders," which was traditionally used in reference to monastic orders, now applying it to the various callings or "walks of life" within the three estates. Holy orders are now not confined to works within a religious order—being a priest, monk, or nun—but embrace also the "secular" stations of life such as life in the civic community (citizenship) and the household (family and work).

In the Small Catechism, the three estates are parsed in this way:

# CHURCH

## *TO BISHOPS, PASTORS, AND PREACHERS*

Here Luther cites texts from the Pastoral Epistles that speak both to the character and capacity of the office-bearer. First Timothy 3:2–4 is prescriptive of the pastor's life as he is to be above ethical reproach, demonstrating fidelity in his marriage and being a good father. Greed, drunkenness, and contentiousness disqualify a man from the pastoral office.[173] First Timothy 3:6 is included to make the point that a man is not be put into the office who is a novice in the faith, lest spiritual pride (conceit) bring about his downfall.[174] Titus 1:9 requires that pastors be faithful to sound doctrine. If the pastor does not hold fast to the trustworthy words of doctrine, he is not equipped to encourage the saints in faith or to defend them against false and pernicious teaching.[175]

---

173    In this and other texts in the Pastoral Epistles, it should be kept in mind that Paul is not giving a complete or comprehensive definition of qualifications necessary for the pastoral office. Robert W. Yarbrough helpfully observes, "He [Paul] gives more of an inner-office memo than a polished employment ad or job description. This format reminds the reader that the traits called for are abbreviated and representative. Much more could be said. Modern readers should not let the smoothed-out and expanded English wording make them forget that Paul is only listing key reference points, not furnishing a full, balanced, and complete statement," in *The Pillar New Testament Commentary: The Letters to Timothy and Titus* (Grand Rapids: Eerdmans, 2018), 193.

174    In his lectures on 1 Timothy, Luther notes: "We have treated this passage 'not [as] a novice' and have said that we must relate it not only to age but also to doctrine. You see, those who are newcomers to the doctrine of the Gospel have not yet been trained and mortified, as is necessary for one who should teach usefully. Those men are crude, unmortified. They are delighted by a fervor for glory" (AE 28:292). Here also see the observation by Elmore Leske: "One reason why a neophyte is not to be entrusted with the office of pastor is supplied by the apostle. One who is immature in the Christian faith is too prone to fall into the most dangerous sin of all: pride," in *The Pastoral Letters* of The Chi Rho Commentary Series (Adelaide, Australia: Lutheran Publishing House, 1986), 61.

175    "The feature that is so striking about verse 9 is the occurrence of *three* expressions of orthodox teaching in the church: the sure word . . . as taught . . . sound doctrine. Paul was never afraid to urge proper indoctrination!" (E. Leske, 182).

## WHAT THE HEARERS OWE THEIR PASTORS

Just as there are divine expectations for those who hold the preaching office, so also are there responsibilities in the congregation for those who hear the Word of God. Hearers of God's Word should provide a salary for preachers of God's Word. This is a command of the Lord (1 Corinthians 9:14).[176] The disciple should share all good things (including financial support) with those who teach (Galatians 6:6–7). Office-bearers deserve both respect and a decent wage (1 Timothy 5:17–18). Respect and honor are to be shown those who are overseers of God's flock, laboring in the Lord (1 Thessalonians 5:12–13). Because pastors preach God's Word, they are to be obeyed as they do this so that their work will not be a burden but a joy (Hebrews 13:17).[177]

# CIVIC COMMUNITY

## OF CIVIL GOVERNMENT

Here Luther cites Romans 13:1–4, where the apostle Paul speaks of everyone submitting to the governing authorities. These authorities are not arbitrary impositions or necessary evils. They are established by God, instituted by Him and used as His masks to govern in a fallen creation. Those placed in the secular offices of government carry the sword in order to resist and punish those who do evil. They are to be recognized and respected not

---

176   See Gregory Lockwood: "Those who overzealously or unfairly promote part-time ministry, expecting workers also to be engaged in another line of work, may cause the church to be short-changed. The tone of Paul's words would suggest that ministers have the right to be supported sufficiently to allow them to devote their undivided attention to the work of the Gospel," in *1 Corinthians*, Concordia Commentary (St. Louis: Concordia Publishing House, 2000), 304.

177   This passage is used in the Rite of Ordination, where the congregation is charged then to receive the pastor "according to the Church's public confession . . . as a servant of Christ and minister of Word and Sacrament," *LSB Agenda* (St. Louis: Concordia Publishing House, 2006), 167. In the Hebrews text, John Kleinig notes, "Their leaders are the congregation's pastors, those who speak God's Word to them when they gather for worship. So the call to heed them is a call to heed God's Word as it is spoken to them," in *Hebrews*, Concordia Commentary (St. Louis: Concordia Publishing House, 2017), 711.

on account of their person but in light of the position God has entrusted to them.

> Since a true Christian lives and labors on earth not for himself alone but for his neighbor, he does by the very nature of his spirit even what he himself has no need of, but is needful and useful to his neighbor. Because the sword is most beneficial and necessary for the whole world in order to preserve peace, punish sin, and restrain the wicked, the Christian submits most willingly to the rule of the sword, pays his taxes, honors those in authority, serves, helps, and does all he can to assist the governing authority, that it may continue to function and be held in honor and fear. Although he has no need of these things for himself—to him they are not essential—nevertheless, he concerns himself about what is serviceable and of benefit to others as Paul teaches in Ephesians 5[:21–6:9].

> (AE 45:94)

## Of Citizens

When Jesus is questioned regarding the permissibility of paying taxes, He responds with the directive: "Give to Caesar what is Caesar's, and to God what is God's" (Matthew 22:21). This text, foundational for Luther's understanding of temporal authority is the first passage cited when it comes to the responsibility that disciples have as citizens. Coupled with Romans 13:5–7, the Scriptures demonstrate that the disciple is not exempt from paying taxes, for this revenue supports those who give their full time to governing.

The Christian lives in God's kingdom inwardly and in the world's kingdom outwardly.

Christ himself made this distinction, and summed it all up very nicely when he said in Matthew 22[:21], "Render to Caesar the things that are Caesar's and to God the things that are God's." Now, if the imperial power extended into God's kingdom and authority, and were not something separate, Christ would not have made this distinction. For, as has been said, the soul is not under the authority of Caesar; he can neither teach it nor guide it, neither kill it nor give it life, neither bind it nor loose it, neither judge it nor condemn it, neither hold it fast nor release it. All this he would have to do, had he the authority to command it and to impose laws upon it. But with respect to body, property, and honor he has indeed to do these things, for such matters are under his authority.

(AE 45:111)

Disciples are mandated to pray "for kings and all those in authority, that we may live peaceful and quiet lives in all godliness and holiness." Hence Luther cites 1 Timothy 2:1–3, reminding Christians of our liturgical duty to serve as intercessors on behalf of those who rule over us, making, administering, and judging the laws of the land. Good government is a gift of daily bread for which Jesus teaches His disciples to pray. The inclusion of Titus 3:1 and 1 Peter 2:13–14 serve to echo and reinforce the truth of Paul's argument in Romans 13.

# THE HOUSEHOLD

Luther begins with marriage, for from the union of man and woman new life is created and sustained in the world. "Marriage belongs to the order of creation and not to the order of salvation."[178]

---

178    Holsten Fagerberg, *A New Look at the Lutheran Confessions: 1529–1537*, 291.

Marriage is the foundation not only for the family but also for the larger sphere of domestic life. Work is done in the household for the well-being of the nearest neighbors, those who live under the same roof. But the work that is done in the local household flows out into the whole world to the benefit of more distant neighbors.

## To Husbands

Luther cites two texts here. First Peter 3:7 exhorts husbands to live gently with their wives, treating them with respect "as the weaker partner" but also as co-heirs of "the gracious gift of life" so that their common prayers might not be disrupted. Colossians 3:19 admonishes husbands to love their wives and not be harsh with them. The strength of the husband is not to be used for abuse but for self-sacrificial service of his wife.

## To Wives

Wives are to submit to their husbands as to the Lord (Ephesians 5:2) and follow the example of Sarah, who did right by obeying Abraham (1 Peter 3:5–6).

## To Parents

Ephesians 6:4 is cited as Paul instructs fathers not to provoke their children to disobedience but bring them up in the training and teaching of Christ Jesus.

## To Children

Luther inserts Ephesians 6:1–3 here with its reference to the Fourth Commandment, particularly the promise that is attached to this commandment: "that you may enjoy long life on the earth."[179]

---

179  Bayer observes that Luther speaks of the Fourth Commandment as "the first and greatest" of those commandments that concern the earthly life: "It is related to the place and activity that most undeniably represents my beginning. Thus the fourth commandment is 'the first and greatest' commandment because it relates to that point at which I was called into life by God through my parents—called into the purely physical, yet at the same time social life. After all, human beings are by their very nature cultural beings. As far as my actions are concerned, the fourth commandment is concerned with the same territory, unequivocally with the pre-ethical—the territory that is

## TO WORKERS OF ALL KINDS

In Luther's day, work was typically done in the context of the home. Luther reflects this reality as he includes biblical passages that have to do with work under the household. Ephesians 6:5–8 in its original context had to do with masters and slaves. Luther applies it to workers who discharge their duties not as those who are merely serving an earthly master but as those who are to recognize that their daily work is, in fact, a service rendered to their Lord Jesus Christ.

## TO EMPLOYERS AND SUPERVISORS

Luther here extends the citation of Ephesians 6 to include verse 9. Earthly masters (employers and supervisors) are to treat those under their employ with justice and kindness, for we all stand under a common Master who does not show partiality or favoritism in His dealings with human beings.

## TO YOUTH

First Peter 5:5–6 is cited as the apostle addresses "young men," urging them to be submissive to their elders, demonstrating humility in recognition of the fact that God opposes the proud but exalts the humble.

## TO WIDOWS

Widows are to put their hope in God, forsaking worldly pleasure and turning to Him in continual prayer according to 1 Timothy 5:5–6.

The Reformer intended that these scriptural verses would serve to admonish Christians to faithfulness in their particular offices in the church, the civil community, and the household.

---

completely removed from my own choosing and deciding. I did not choose my parents, the place or language of my birth; I was born. As theological language has it: I was created; God created me into life, albeit, through my parents," in "The Protestant Understanding of Marriage and Family," *Freedom in Response,* 158.

In language reminiscent of the *Confession Concerning Christ's Supper* written in the previous year, Luther concludes this section of the Small Catechism with texts from Romans 13:9, which calls on the disciple to love the neighbor as he or she loves the self, and 1 Timothy 2:1, which urges prayers for all people.

Luther's Table of Duties reflects his doctrine of vocation.[180] Called by the Gospel to faith in Christ, we now live in the favor of the Father. Good works do not save, and the Father in heaven does not need them, but my neighbor certainly needs them. Given the fact that the old Adam never ceases to determine for himself the works that he believes will bring self-fulfillment and make him acceptable to God, Luther directs disciples to God's commands that identify the works that are pleasing to God when done in faith. Disciples do not determine for themselves which works will please God nor the time and place they are to be done. God has instituted these three estates, or places, of life. They are the arenas where faith is active in love. Precisely within these callings, the life of discipleship takes place.

> **Luther's Table of Duties reflects his doctrine of vocation.**

---

180   For more on Luther's doctrine of vocation, see Mark D. Tranvik, *Martin Luther and the Called Life* (Minneapolis: Fortress Press, 2016); Carl Trueman, *Luther and the Christian Life: Cross and Freedom* (Wheaton: Crossway Books, 2015); and especially the classic by Gustaf Wingren, *Luther on Vocation,* trans. Carl C. Rasmussen (Philadelphia: Muhlenberg Press, 1957).

## FOR FURTHER REFLECTION AND STUDY: CONNECTIONS WITH LUTHER'S SMALL CATECHISM WITH EXPLANATION 2017

1. How were "holy orders" understood in the Medieval Church? (See p. 349.)

2. How did Luther come to understand "holy orders" in a radically different way? (See p. 349.)

3. Read 1 Timothy 3:2–4 and Titus 1:9. What are God's vocational expectations for those who serve in the pastoral office? (See p. 349.)

4. Read 1 Thessalonians 5:12–13 and Hebrews 13:17. How are hearers of God's Word to relate to servants of the Word? (See p. 349.)

5. Read 1 Corinthians 9:14; Galatians 6:6–7; 1 Timothy 5:17–18. What financial obligations do disciples have to those called to be their shepherds? (See p. 349.)

6. How does the Fourth Commandment inform our understanding of Romans 13:1–4; Matthew 22:21; Romans 13:5–7; 1 Timothy 2:1–3; Titus 3:1; and 1 Peter 2:13–14? (See pp. 349–50.)

7. Read 1 Peter 3:7; Colossians 3:19; Ephesians 5:22; and 1 Peter 3:5–6. What do these texts teach us about God's design for the discipleship of men and women in marriage? (See p. 350.)

8. Read Ephesians 6:5–8. We no longer live in a world of masters and slaves. How does this passage apply to relationships in the workplace? (See p. 350.)

9. Read Romans 13:9 and 1 Timothy 2:1. How do these two texts summarize the stance of the disciple in the world? (See p. 350.)

# Appendix

# Catechesis for Life in the Royal Priesthood[181]

In spite of numerous adamic attempts to put the Lord Jesus Christ in the unemployment office and take over his work with blueprints for the building of the church according to our own schemes and tools of our making, the Lord Jesus Christ alone remains the architect and builder of his church. In those regal words of St. Matthew 16:18 he says, "I will build my church, and the gates of hell shall not prevail against it." This same Lord, now crucified and raised from the dead, speaks with all authority on the day of his Ascension, giving to his disciples the mandate to make disciples of all nations by baptizing them in the name of the Father and of the Son and of the Holy Spirit and teaching them to keep all that he has given us. Disciples are made by baptizing and teaching. Jesus builds his church with these tools. This teaching that flows from Holy Baptism and leads to Holy Baptism is catechesis. Catechesis is the way in which the word of God is spoken and then echoes back in confession to the glory of the Father, Son, and Holy Spirit.

Catechesis is concerned with "faith development" but in a way that is fundamentally opposed to the theory of faith development set forth by James Fowler in his books *Stages of Faith* and *Becoming*

181    John T. Pless, "Catechesis for Life in the Royal Priesthood," in *Logia: A Journal of Lutheran Theology* 3, no. 4 (Reformation 1994), 3–10. Reprinted with permission. This paper was originally presented by the author at pastoral conferences in the Iowa District East and the Southern Illinois District (LCMS) in April 1994.

*Adult, Becoming Christian.*[182] Fowler posits a movement through seven stages of faith, beginning with what he calls "primal faith" moving toward the ultimate "universalizing faith." The stages of faith according to Fowler evolve from a lower to higher form with very few individuals ever achieving "universalizing faith," which would be represented in such figures as Gandhi and Martin Luther King standing as examples of tolerant inclusivity. The faith development theorists work with the assumption that faith is brought to maturity by moving people beyond the community, enabling them to stand as autonomous selves over against any particular narrative.

Lutheran catechesis, however, proceeds from an altogether different orientation. The goal of our catechesis is to shape the baptized to live in Christ as members of the Royal Priesthood. Catechesis does not result in the formation of the autonomous spiritual ego, but in a priest living in the company of fellow priests under a common High Priest and sharing in a common cultus. Fowler's "stages of faith model" is a secularized form of Pietism.

> **The goal of our catechesis is to shape the baptized to live in Christ as members of the Royal Priesthood.**

Catechesis is the process of transmitting the word of God so that the mind and life of the one who receives it grows up in every way into Jesus Christ, living in faith toward him and in love toward the neighbor. While catechesis does lead from the font to the altar, culminating in the extolling of the Lord's gifts and the confession of his name in that churchly rite called Confirmation, catechesis itself is from the womb to the tomb. Catechesis has a text and a context. The text is the Small Catechism and the context is the Royal Priesthood, the holy church.

We turn first to the text. Beginning in 1518, Luther frequently preached series of sermons on the Catechism, that is, the basic

---

182    See James Fowler, *Stages of Faith* (San Francisco: Harper & Row, 1981) and *Becoming Adult, Becoming Christian* (San Francisco: Harper & Row, 1984). Fowler's approach has been widely used by a variety of theorists in Christian education. For an example, see Thomas Groome, *Christian Religious Education* (San Francisco: Harper & Row, 1980).

components of Christian doctrine as they had been arranged and handed down from earlier generations of Christians. As early as 1525, Luther had expressed his concern that a good catechism be prepared for the instruction of the young in the evangelical faith. In a letter addressed to Nicholas Hausmann on February 2, 1525, Luther notes that Agricola and Jonas had been given the task of preparing such a catechism. This catechism, however, never materialized. The Saxon Visitations of 1528 revealed such spiritual disorder in the congregations that Luther himself was compelled to prepare both of the Catechisms, Small and Large.

Commenting on the visitations, Luther writes in the Preface to the Small Catechism:

> The deplorable conditions that I repeatedly encountered when I was a visitor constrained me to prepare this brief and simple catechism or statement of Christian teaching. Good God, what wretchedness I beheld! The common people, especially those who live in the country, have no knowledge whatever of Christian teaching, and unfortunately many pastors are quite incompetent and unfitted for teaching. Although the people are supposed to be Christian, are baptized, and receive the holy sacrament, they do not know the Lord's Prayer, the Creed, or the Ten Commandments, they live as though they were pigs and irrational beasts, and now that the gospel has been restored they have mastered the fine art of abusing liberty.
>
> (SC PREFACE, 1–3)

Luther intended his catechisms as a remedy to this crisis in the church.

In Luther's mind, the Small Catechism was a text for use not so much in the classroom as in the home. This is revealed in the heading that stands over each of the chief parts: "in the plain form in which the head of the family shall teach them to his household."

Historically, it was the Small Catechism that was crystallized from the Large Catechism. H. Bornkamm notes, "Without the preparatory condensation of the catechetical sermons into the Large Catechism, there would have been no crystallization of the entire substance into the Small Catechism."[183] The Large Catechism is an exposition of the Small Catechism for pastors, teachers, and other adult Christians to assist them in teaching the Small Catechism.

We would do well to remember that the Preface to the Small Catechism is also part of the confessional corpus. In it we see Luther's theory of catechesis. In the Preface, Luther makes three major points that are crucial to evangelical catechesis. First, there should be a standard and fixed text. Luther writes, "In the first place, the preacher should take the utmost care to avoid changes or variations in the text and the wording of the Ten Commandments, the Creed, the Lord's Prayer, the sacraments, etc. On the contrary, he should adopt one form, adhere to it, and use it repeatedly year after year. Young and inexperienced people must be instructed on the basis of a uniform, fixed text and form. They are easily confused if a teacher employs one form now and another form—perhaps with the intention of making improvements later on . . . when you are teaching the young, adhere to a fixed and unchanging form and method. Begin by teaching them the Ten Commandments, the Creed, the Lord's Prayer, etc., following the text word for word so that the young may repeat these things after you and retain them in their memory" (SC, Preface, 7, 9–10).

Second, Luther argues that the catechist should move from text to meaning. Luther comments, "After the people have become familiar with the text, teach them what it means" (SC, Preface, 14).

Third, the text of the Catechism is never exhausted. There is always more to learn, so Luther advises that "after you have thus

---

183    Heinrich Bornkamm, *Luther in Mid-Career, 1521–1530*, trans. E. Theodore Bachmann (Philadelphia: Fortress Press, 1983), 601. On the genesis of the Catechisms, also see Martin Brecht, *Martin Luther: Shaping and Defining the Reformation 1521–1532*, trans. James Schaaf (Minneapolis: Fortress Press, 1990), 273–79; J. M. Reu, *Dr. Martin Luther's Small Catechism: A History*, 7–24; Timothy J. Wengert, "Wittenberg's Earliest Catechism," in *Lutheran Quarterly* (Autumn 1993): 247–60.

taught this brief catechism, take up a larger catechism so that the people may have a richer and fuller understanding" (SC, Preface, 17).

From Luther's Preface to the Small Catechism, it is apparent that he envisioned this book to be far more than a miniature textbook in systematic theology. For Luther, the Catechism is the handbook of doctrine, prayer, and life. As a handbook of Christian doctrine, the Small Catechism is confession, that is, a repeating back to God what he has said to us in the Holy Scriptures. James Voelz calculates that approximately one-fourth of the Small Catechism is direct quotation from the Scriptures, another one-third is direct exposition of the biblical text, while the remainder is application of scriptural teaching to life.[184] The Catechism summarizes Scripture and leads us back into Scripture. A sixteenth-century Lutheran by the name of Christopher Fischer declared,

> Just as the best, most experienced alchemist draws forth the quintessence, that is, the core, power, sap, and pitch of a thing, so God in his great mercy has prepared in the precious Catechism an extract, an excerpt, a brief summary and epitome of the entire Holy Scripture for people who are thirsty and hungry for grace. In the Catechism he has brought together in clear and distinct words which everyone can understand everything a Christian needs to know and to believe for his salvation. If a teaching agrees with the precious Catechism, every Christian may accept it in good conscience.[185]

The Formula of Concord speaks of the Small Catechism as the "layman's Bible," confessing that it "contains everything that Holy Scripture discusses at greater length and which a Christian must know for his salvation" (FC, Ep., 5). The Small Catechism

---

184    James Voelz, "Luther's Use of Scripture in the Small Catechism," in *Luther's Catechisms—450 Years*, eds. Robert Preus and David Scaer (Fort Wayne: Concordia Theological Seminary, 1979), 55.

185    Quoted by Robert Kolb, "The Laymen's Bible: The Use of Luther's Catechisms in the German Late Reformation," in Preus and Scaer, 16.

——✦·✦—✦·✦——

**The Formula of Concord speaks of the Small Catechism as the "layman's Bible,".**

——✦·✦—✦·✦——

is not a substitute for the Scriptures, but, to use the imagery of Charles Arand, "a map for the study of Scripture."[186] Occasionally one hears the complaint that Lutherans replace the Bible with the Catechism or that Lutherans know the Catechism but don't know the Bible. These criticisms, it seems to me, miss the point. The Bible is a big book, and if one resolves to read the Scriptures, he is launching out on a journey that is beset with potential dangers. Witness how many sincere Bible readers misread the holy text and are led away from Jesus Christ.

We are Evangelical Lutherans, not Fundamentalists. Among other things, that means it is not the presence of the Bible that locates the church and brings people to faith, but rather "the church is the assembly of saints in which the gospel is taught purely and the sacraments are administered rightly" (AC VII, 1–2). The emphasis is on the preaching of the pure gospel and the right administration of the sacraments. Lutherans of the old Synodical Conference have spent a lot of time and energy defending the inerrancy of the Scriptures, and I do not deny that this was a necessary battle. But could it be that in the battle over the Bible we have forgotten that it is not enough to talk about characteristics of the Bible—inerrant, infallible, and inspired? The question still remains: how will the Holy Scriptures be read and proclaimed? Will the law be properly distinguished from the gospel? Will the Scriptures be interpreted in accordance with the mind of the Spirit who inspired them, or will biblical interpretation move according to the impulse of the interpreter?

Here the Small Catechism proves itself to be a reliable road map that our youth need to learn if they are to chart their course in the Scriptures in such a way that always leads to the morning

---

186    Charles P. Arand, "Luther's Catechisms: Maps for the Study of Scripture," *Issues in Christian Education* (Summer 1990): 22. In this connection, also see Paul I. Johnston, "Reu's Understanding of the Small Catechism," *Lutheran Quarterly* (Winter 1993): 425–50.

star, Jesus Christ (2 Peter 1:19). The Catechism, then, may be described as that "pattern of sound words" which Timothy is exhorted to follow in 2 Timothy 1:13. Therefore, the Small Catechism is to be understood not merely as a collection of essential doctrines, but as the very pattern or shape of Christian doctrine. As a handbook of Christian doctrine, the Small Catechism has a particular theological structure that moves from law to gospel. The ordering of the six chief parts is not accidental but expresses the dynamics of biblical teaching. The structure of the Small Catechism, the sequence of its chief parts, is crucial to a right understanding of Luther's theological intent in catechesis, as Robert Schultz has demonstrated.[187]

> The Catechism, then, may be described as that "pattern of sound words" which Timothy is exhorted to follow in 2 Timothy 1:13.

A reordering or rearrangement of the chief parts of the Small Catechism signals a change in theological focus. Agricola would have us begin with the Creed, that is, the gospel. Here we may recall the Antinomian controversy and the impetus that it provided toward the "Articles of Visitation" of 1528. Some contemporary recastings of the Small Catechism would have the catechesis begin with Holy Baptism. Others, under Barthian influence, would place a great deal of weight on the prologue to the Ten Commandments of Exodus 20:2, "I am the Lord your God, who brought you out of the land of Egypt, out of the house of bondage," as a "gospel" preface to the law.

We are not Jews. The Ten Commandments were not given to us, but we are not without the law. Luther omits the biblical prologue and states the brute fact of God's law, spoken to Jew and Gentile alike (e.g., Romans 1): "You shall have no other gods before me." This law exposes and executes the sinner, who lacks

---

187    Robert Schultz, "The Theological Significance of the Order of the Chief Parts in Luther's Catechism," in *Teaching the Faith: Luther's Catechisms in Perspective*, ed. Carl Volz (River Forest: Lutheran Education Association, 1967), 45–46.

the fear, love, and trust in God above all things. The center of gravity for Luther's catechesis of the law is located in the First Commandment, as is demonstrated in the Large Catechism.

The Apostles' Creed follows the Decalogue as the gospel follows the law. Breaking from medieval tradition, Luther understood the Creed as a Trinitarian confession of the gospel to be interpreted christologically. Both the Father and his gifts in creation and the Spirit and his gifts that create and sustain faith are confessed in their relationship to the Son. The Our Father is prayed in response to the Creed—it is the prayer of faith. The gifts of redemption confessed in the Second Article of the Creed are concretely given in Holy Baptism, Holy Absolution, and the Sacrament of the Altar.

The prayers and the table of duties form appendices to the six chief parts of the Christian doctrine, but that does not mean that they are excluded from the theological structure of the Small Catechism. On the contrary, they demonstrate how the Catechism's doctrine shapes the believer's life—a life of doxology that prays within the rhythm of time (morning, evening, and at meals) and works within the structures of this world (congregation, civil realm, family, and occupation).

Catechesis has a context, the royal priesthood of believers. Debates regarding "church and ministry" in the nineteenth

> **Catechesis has a context, the royal priesthood of believers.**

century have perhaps clouded the fact that the primary distinction in 1 Peter 2:1–10 is not an anticlerical distinction between those who are called and ordained into the office of the holy ministry and the rest of the baptized, but between faith and unfaith. The church is a priesthood, and within that priesthood there is an office established by God himself to provide oversight for the spiritual house that God has built. All believers are priests, but not all priests are ministers. 1 Peter 2:1–10 is descriptive of the identity and activity of the royal priesthood.

The 1 Peter text has often been used as a polemic against the Roman Catholic conception of the priesthood—that is, since Jesus Christ is our High Priest we do not need a human priest as a mediator between God and the Christian. As each believer is a priest, he or she may go directly to God. Such a use of the text misses the point that the holy apostle makes. We are not a collection of isolated priests, each doing our own thing before God. Rather Peter says that we are "built into a spiritual house, to be a holy priesthood" (1 Peter 2:5) and that we are "a chosen race, a royal priesthood, a holy nation, God's own people" (1 Peter 2:9). George Wollenburg writes,

> A race is more than a collection of individuals. A race has identity that is derived from a common ancestry. You cannot join a race, you are born into it. The chosen race has a Father in heaven and a mother on earth—Holy Church. Her members are born of water and the Spirit (John 3:5). Their mother is the holy and pure bride of Christ, the Church (Gal 4:26; Eph 5:25–27; Rev 12:1, 5–6; Is 66:8–9). This race is a spiritual house (1 Peter 2:5) in the sense of the royal "house" or lineage.[188]

Priests in this priesthood get their identity from the name put upon them in Holy Baptism: Father, Son, and Holy Spirit. In Holy Baptism, God makes us priests in his priesthood. F. L. Cross, among others, has suggested that 1 Peter is a baptismal document originally associated with Easter baptisms in the early church.[189] Whether or not this hypothesis is correct, 1 Peter was surely written with Holy Baptism in view. Not only does 1 Peter provide us with one of the key baptismal texts in the New Testament in 3:21 ("Baptism now saves you"); the whole epistle

---

188    George Wollenburg in an unpublished essay, "The Priesthood of Believers as It Relates to the Divine Service." Also see Erling Teigen, "The Universal Priesthood in the Lutheran Confessions," in *Logia* (Reformation 1992): 9–16.

189    See Frank Cross, *1 Peter: A Paschal Liturgy* (London: SPCK, 1954).

is, in fact, derived from the Father's mercy by which "we have been born anew to a living hope through the resurrection of Jesus Christ from the dead" (1:13). This new birth was brought about not by "perishable seed but of imperishable, through the living and abiding word of God" (1:23). Baptism sets us apart as "aliens and exiles" to live as members of God's holy priesthood.

Priests in this priesthood do three things: (1) Priests offer sacrifices; (2) priests speak to other people on behalf of God; and (3) priests speak to God on behalf of other people. Catechesis is the training that Christians are given for this priestly life and work.

Priests offer sacrifices. What are these sacrifices? As Article XXIV of the Apology reminds us, there is a singular propitiatory sacrifice, and that is the death of our High Priest, Jesus Christ. The Apology goes on to confess that all other sacrifices are eucharistic sacrifices. "The rest are eucharistic sacrifices, called 'sacrifices of praise': the proclamation of the gospel, faith, prayer, thanksgiving, confession, the affliction of the saints, yes, all good works of the saints. . . . The sacrifices of the New Testament are of this type, as Peter teaches in 1 Peter 2:5, 'A holy priesthood, to offer spiritual sacrifices.' Spiritual sacrifices are contrasted not only with the sacrifices of cattle but also with human works offered *ex opere operato*, for 'spiritual' refers to the operation of the Holy Spirit within us" (AP XXIV, 25–26).

Priests offer the daily sacrifice of repentance. Indeed, David tells us in Psalm 51 that "the sacrifices of God are a broken spirit, a broken and contrite heart." In the royal priesthood, repentance is not a religious exercise that one engages in only to move on to some other aspect of the Christian life. Repentance is the Christian life. Or as Luther said in the first of his Ninety-Five Theses, "When our Lord and Master Jesus Christ said 'repent' (Mt 4:17), he willed the entire life of believers to be one of repentance."[190] The catechesis embodied in the Small Catechism sets the life of the Christian

---

190    AE 31:25.

in the rhythm of repentance, daily dying to sin and being made alive to walk in the newness of life.

The sacrifice of repentance is the sacrifice of one's own life. In Romans 12:1–2, St. Paul writes, "I beseech you therefore, brethren, by the mercies of God, that you present your bodies as a living sacrifice, holy, acceptable to God, which is your reasonable service. And do not be conformed to this world, but be transformed by the renewing of your mind, that you may prove what is that good and acceptable and perfect will of God" (Rom 12:1–2 NKJV).

Here the apostle puts two words together in a way that must have jarred his original readers: sacrifice and living. Everybody in the ancient world knew that sacrifices were dead! Goats and bulls were slaughtered in a temple that resembled a meat packing house more than a church, by a priest who could pass for a butcher. Whether you were Jewish or pagan, you knew that sacrifices were killed. But in the vocabulary of the Holy Spirit, "living sacrifice" is no oxymoron. Romans 3 notes that the death of Jesus Christ is the atoning sacrifice for sin. In Romans 6, Paul maintains that we were joined to that death in our Baptism, and sharing in the Lord's death we are also made partakers of his resurrection. Hence in Romans 12 the Apostle beseeches us to present our bodies as a living sacrifice.

Luther and the Lutheran Confessions removed sacrifice from the chancel and relocated it in the world, as the whole life of the believer becomes a living sacrifice. This is "the liturgy after the liturgy," to borrow a phrase from Carter Lindberg.[191] Served with the gifts of the gospel in the Divine Service, the life of worship is lived out in the concrete

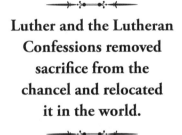

**Luther and the Lutheran Confessions removed sacrifice from the chancel and relocated it in the world.**

---

191   Carter Lindberg, *Beyond Charity* (Minneapolis: Fortress Press, 1993), 169. Also see Robert Kolb, *Teaching God's Children His Teaching: A Guide for the Study of Luther's Catechism* (Hutchinson, MN: Crown Publishing, 1992), 8:1–8:14; Harold Senkbeil, *Sanctification: Christ in Action* (Milwaukee: Northwestern Publishing House, 1989), 111–48.

places of our various callings. The Small Catechism connects sanctification—the life of the living sacrifice—with vocation.

Priests speak to people on behalf of God. The life of the royal priesthood is doxological in word and deed. Notice the description in Hebrews 13: "Therefore by him let us continually offer the sacrifice of praise to God, that is the fruit of our lips, giving thanks to his name. But do not forget to do good and to share, for with such sacrifices God is well pleased" (Heb 13:15–16 NKJV). The language here is not unlike the language of 1 Peter 2:9–10 where God's people declare the wonderful deeds of the God who called us out of darkness into his marvelous light. The language of the Old Testament cultus has shaped these passages. Sinners brought into the presence of a Holy God by his grace now render thanks to him by confessing what God has done. Confession is doxology.

Again catechesis tutors us in such doxology. The Apostles' Creed recites "the wonderful deeds of God who called us out of darkness into his marvelous light."

The Creed is the yardstick for measuring our speech about God. If one is going to talk about God as a member of his priesthood and not as a gossip, his language about him must square with these words.

Priests speak to God on behalf of people. This is the priestly work of intercession. "Let my prayer be set before you as incense; the lifting up of my hands as the evening sacrifice" (Ps 141:2). Praying priests come before the Father in faith, and in love they lift the needs of the neighbor to him in whose name alone there is help. Here the Small Catechism functions as our prayerbook. It was Wilhelm Loehe who noted that of all the catechisms within Christendom, the Small Catechism alone was capable of being prayed.[192]

We have outlined rather broadly the identity and life of the royal priesthood that is gathered by the High Priest, Jesus Christ,

---

192   Wilhelm Loehe, *Three Books About the Church*, trans. James Schaaf (Philadelphia: Fortress Press, 1969), 170.

by his word and sacraments. We now turn to the catechesis that goes on within this royal priesthood.

Something is wrong. We have all heard the statistics of the number of youth who drop out of the church after confirmation. We know that confirmation is to be seen in light of Holy Baptism and not vice versa. We know that confirmation is not graduation from catechesis. Yet what pastor has not experienced some degree of frustration and disappointment when it comes to the instruction of the youth and their subsequent confirmation?

In 1966, a pan-Lutheran commission was assembled to study the theology and practice of confirmation. After having collected data from 86,000 participants, the Joint Commission prepared a study entitled *A Report on the Study of Confirmation and First Communion* in 1969. Among other things, this study suggested that confirmation be separated from first communion, with first communion taking place around the fifth grade. The recommendations of the report were widely accepted and implemented in the ALC and LCA, but much less so in the LCMS. While it is beyond the scope of this paper to assess the inter-Lutheran report, a few observations are in order. First, early communion with confirmation coming later does not appear to reverse the trend of adolescents falling away from active participation in congregational life in the ELCA. Second, the report continued to view catechesis as primarily an educational process rather than training for life in the royal priesthood. Third, the report tended to downplay the significance of the Small Catechism in catechesis. This final trend effected both catechetical curriculum and recastings of the Rite of Confirmation.

Walter Carlson of the former LCA, writing in the Winter 1982 issue of *Dialog* in an article "LCA Catechesis The Reformation Lost," critiques his church body's catechetical curriculum, *Catechetics For Today*, concluding, "I entitled the essay 'LCA Catechesis—The Reformation Lost' because I failed to recognize in this material the fundamental insights of the Reformation.

While familiar terms from Lutheran theology and catechetical tradition are employed, the methodology and theological content are foreign to anything I have come to understand as Lutheran."[193] Virgil Thompson makes similar observations about more recent catechetical practices in the ELCA in "The Promise of Catechesis" in the Autumn 1990 issue of the *Lutheran Quarterly*, lamenting that

> **In the place of the classical service of catechesis as indoctrination to the dogma of the church and introduction to the discipline of theological reflection, one hears of the pastor who ushers his confirmation class into the darkened sanctuary, instructs the students to close their eyes, and get in touch with their spirituality. While such a silly approach to teaching the faith may be an isolated incidence, the aversion to catechesis as indoctrination to dogma, which lies behind it, is not isolated. This understanding of catechesis is widely abandoned throughout the church. In this sense the church seems to be intent on chasing the epistemological train which just left the station and wrecked a few miles down the track.[194]**

The rite entitled "Affirmation of Baptism" in the *Lutheran Book of Worship* has no mention of instruction in the Small Catechism or of a confession of the Christian faith normed by this document.

Frustration over confirmation instruction has led to a lot of tinkering with programs, techniques, and in the case of the *Lutheran Book of Worship*, the very structure of the Rite of Confirmation itself, but we are still left with an inadequate view of catechesis. I have no sure-fire programs to suggest or techniques to teach that would stop the post-confirmation exodus. I am only urging that we reclaim the Small Catechism as the handbook for our catechesis and the royal priesthood as the context for the catechesis.

---

193   Walter Carlson, "LCA Catechesis—The Reformation Lost," in *Dialog* (Winter 1982): 13.

194   Virgil Thompson, "The Promise of Catechesis," in *Lutheran Quarterly* (Autumn 1990): 264.

The royal priesthood as the context for catechesis has three dimensions: (1) The royal priesthood lives under the oversight of the Pastoral Office, and that office is primarily a teaching office; (2) catechesis is more than the classroom; (3) catechesis cannot be divorced from the Divine Service.

The royal priesthood lives under the oversight of the Pastoral Office, and that office is primarily a teaching office. I do not take the reference in Ephesians 4:11 to "pastors and teachers" to be a reference to two separate offices but to one office. As Bertil Gaertner has pointed out in his paper "Didaskolos: Men, Women, and the Office in the New Testament," the pastor shepherds the congregation by his authoritative teaching.[195] The pastor is the teacher. There may be other catechists in the congregation, but they serve under the supervision of the pastor, who is given responsibility for the teaching that goes on within the congregation.

Under the impact of modernity there are significant pressures brought to bear on the pastoral office that would make the office something other than the teaching office of the church. Alistar MacIntyre has argued that modernity has produced a world view that is managerial and therapeutic. Os Guinness in his excellent book *Dining with the Devil: The Megachurch Movement Flirts with Modernity* maintains that the managerial and therapeutic approaches spawned by modernity have subjected the gospel to the pragmatism of "whatever works" and to the subjectivity of whatever therapy brings relief.[196] Thus the pastor is seen as a CEO, a shopkeeper catering to ill-defined spiritual needs, or a rancher. In *The Parish Paper* Lyle Schaller writes, "The most difficult and certainly the most demanding change is for the minister to move from the stance of pastor, teacher, shepherd, to becoming a skilled and effective agent of intentional change."[197] The managerial model

---

195    Bertil Gaertner, "Didaskolos: The Office, Man and Woman in the New Testament," in *Concordia Journal* (March 1982): 52–60.

196    See Os Guinness, *Dining with the Devil: The Megachurch Movement Flirts with Modernity* (Grand Rapids: Baker Book House, 1993).

197    Lyle Schaller, *The Parish Paper* (April 1988), 1.

would subordinate the pastor as shepherd/teacher to the pastor as administrator.

The ascendancy of the therapeutic model is traced by E. Brooks Holifield in his book *From Salvation to Self-Realization: The History of Pastoral Care in America*.[198] Actually, the title says it all. Brooks charts the evolution of pastoral care that was centered in the language of prayer and Scripture in the early American Puritans to the contemporary paradigm embodied in the Clinical Pastoral Care Movement.

The catechesis of the Small Catechism cannot be sustained by either of these models. Yes, there are budgets to be managed and broken lives to be mended. There are others in the congregation who can attend to many of these things. Recall that the apostles appointed seven men to take care of the food distribution program so that the apostles could devote themselves "to prayer and to the ministry of the word" (Acts 6:4). In the present-day church we often do just the opposite, as pastors turn over "prayer and . . . the ministry of the word" to the laity and instead busy themselves with the multiplication of programs and administration of parish business.

Let the pastors teach. Especially let the pastor teach the adults. James Smart was fond of saying that our Lord blessed the children and taught the adults and that we have turned it around so that we teach the children and bless the adults. The catechesis envisioned by Luther, following the lead of Deuteronomy 6, would have the "head of the household" teaching the Small Catechism to his family. If parents are going to be the primary catechists, then they will need to be taught by the pastor in adult Bible classes, retreats, and other formal settings, but also in informal settings as the pastor visits in the home or counsels with couples preparing for marriage or awaiting the birth of a child.

---

198    See E. Brooks Holifield, *From Salvation to Self-Realization: The History of Pastoral Care in America* (Nashville: Abingdon Press, 1983).

That leads to the second dimension: Catechesis is not confined to the classroom. In a very provocative article under the title "Catechesis: The Quiet Crisis," William Thompson observes:

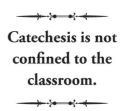

**Catechesis is not confined to the classroom.**

> For Luther, the Catechism is a prayerbook, not merely a book of doctrine. The Catechism is an enchiridion, a handbook for living the baptismal life. Catechesis is the training in living as a baptized child of God, not just the accumulation of facts. The central error that we have made in catechesis is to treat it as an academic process rather than our patterning of living in our baptism. We have treated the Catechism as a textbook rather than a prayerbook. Consequently, many adults, including pastors, view the Catechism as a book for children and not for us, as if it were a book like other school books—something to be tolerated until graduation and then discarded. This problem is further compounded when pastors who do seek to use the Catechism concentrate on explanations of the Catechism rather than on the Catechism itself.[199]

As we have already noted, catechesis is from the womb to the tomb, and the Small Catechism is to be the Christian's handbook not merely for a couple of years but for a lifetime. Such catechesis can be fleshed out in the congregation in a number of ways. Pastors will need to continue to study and pray the Catechism. Listen to the admonition of Luther in the Preface to the Large Catechism:

> To our regret we see that even many pastors are neglectful of the Catechism, despising both their office and the Catechism itself. . . . As for myself, let me say this: I, too, am a doctor and pastor. In fact, I am as

---

199   William Thompson, "Catechesis: The Quiet Crisis," in *The Bride of Christ* (Advent 1990), 22.

educated and experienced as any of those who have all that nerve and brazen self-confidence. Yet I continue to do as a child does that is being taught the Catechism. Mornings and whenever I have time I recite word for word and pray the Ten Commandments, the creed, etc. I must still study and pray the catechism daily, yet I cannot master it as I would like, but must remain a child and student of the catechism. This I do gladly. But those who think they have mastered it in one reading need not anticipate failing; they have already failed. What they need to do is to become children again and start learning their ABC's, which they falsely imagine they long ago had under their belts.

(LC, MARTIN LUTHER'S PREFACE, I, 7–8)

Pastors will need to use a variety of means to help their people make use of the Small Catechism. When a child is baptized, present the parents with a copy of the Small Catechism inscribed for the child with words something like this: "Today God washed your sin away in the waters of Holy Baptism and made you a priest in his holy and royal priesthood. This Catechism is your handbook for life in God's priesthood. Your parents will use this book to help you understand what God did for you today in your baptism and how you are to live as his child." Encourage the parents to use the Small Catechism as a prayerbook in family devotions and to help their children learn the six chief parts by heart long before they come to catechetical instruction in the seventh grade.

Pastors are not marriage counselors but shepherds of Christ's flock. The Small Catechism used in conjunction with the marriage liturgy from the *Lutheran Worship Agenda* are biblical and churchly means for helping engaged couples look at marriage as an estate formed by God for their good and blessing.

Preach catechetical sermons. The six midweek services in the Lenten Season provide an excellent opportunity to preach sermons on the six chief parts of the Small Catechism. The lectionary often is directly linked to one of the chief parts of the Small Catechism, thus providing yet another opportunity for catechetical preaching.

The third dimension of catechesis has to do with the Divine Service. Philip Lee writes: "The liturgy of the church, after all, served as the training ground for Christians for centuries before the Protestant Sunday School was invented."[200]

The Divine Service (subjective genitive) is the Lord's service to us. Luke 22:24–30 is an excellent text to use to teach the Divine Service, for here in the context of the institution of the Sacrament of the Altar our Lord says, "I am among you as one who serves" (Luke 22:27). The Lord of heaven and earth clothed in our flesh and blood becomes our Host and Servant. The liturgy is not a service we render to God, but his service to us by means of his saving word and blessed sacrament.

In this Divine Service there is ongoing catechesis, week after week and year after year. There is built into the liturgy a blessed sameness. As C. S. Lewis says, a good liturgy is like a well-worn pair of shoes. . . . By repetition of the Kyrie, the Gloria, the Creed, the Our Father, the Sanctus, and the Agnus Dei we commit these treasures drawn from God's Word to heart. We become at home with them and yet never exhaust their riches.

The liturgy provides a deep structure for catechesis as it embraces us in the Lord's name. The proclamation of the Lord's name in the invocation locates us in Holy Baptism. Baptism is not a past event but a present reality, as the Lord into whose name we have been baptized says: "Lo, I am with you always" (Matthew 28:20). Baptism plunges us into a daily death of contrition and repentance. This is liturgically indicated by the placement of Confession and Absolution immediately after the baptismal name of God. Absolved of our sins, we come into the courts of the Lord's house with words of praise and thanks that we have received from him in the Introit. The Lord's word is read and preached. On the

---

200    Philip Lee, *Against the Protestant Gnostics* (New York: Oxford, 1987), 228.

basis of the Lord's speaking to us we speak to him in prayer. The Lord serves us with his body and blood. With his name put on us in the Benediction, we are sent back into the world to live as his people, holy and precious in his sight. The Introduction to *Lutheran Worship* is a classic statement of the catechetical value of the Divine Service:

> Our Lord speaks and we listen. His Word bestows what it says. Faith that is born from what is heard acknowledges the gifts received with eager thankfulness and praise. Music is drawn into this thankfulness and praise, enlarging and elevating the adoration of our gracious giver God.
>
> Saying back to him what he has said to us, we repeat what is most true and sure. Most true and sure is his name, which he put upon us with the water of our Baptism. We are his. This we acknowledge at the beginning of the Divine Service. Where his name is, there is he. Before him we acknowledge that we are sinners, and we plead for forgiveness. His forgiveness is given us, and we, freed and forgiven, acclaim him as our great and gracious God as we apply to ourselves the words he had used to make himself known to us.
>
> The rhythm of our worship is from him to us, and then from us back to him. He gives his gifts, and together we receive and extol them. We build one another up as we speak to one another in psalms, hymns, and spiritual songs. Our Lord gives us his body to eat and his blood to drink. Finally his blessing moves us out into our calling, where his gifts have their fruition. How best to do this we may learn from his Word and from the way his Word has prompted his worship through the centuries. We are heirs of an astonishingly rich tradition. Each generation receives from those who went before and, in making that tradition of the Divine Service its own, adds what best

may serve in its own day—the living heritage and something new.[201]

The Divine Service takes place within the context of the Christian year. The church year so clearly and consistently unfolds the life of the Holy Trinity in its various seasons and days. The church year has a "trinitarian shape" that is centered in the death and resurrection of our Lord Jesus Christ (Good Friday and Easter) and expressed in the Time of Christmas (Father), the Time of Easter (Son), and the Time of the Church (Holy Spirit). All of the church year either leads into Good Friday–Easter or flows from Good Friday–Easter. The historic Gospel for the First Sunday in Advent is Luke 19:29–38, the Palm Sunday narrative. Why has the Palm Sunday account been read on the first Sunday of the church year for over a thousand years? Why Palm Sunday, when the world is getting ready for Christmas? The Blessed King who comes in the name of the Lord comes to suffer and die. The first half of the church year is geared to move toward Good Friday and Easter.

This movement continues through Christmas as the Son of God is born in the lowliness of Bethlehem. He becomes incarnate in order to be the sacrifice for sin. Epiphany makes manifest both his person and his work. The Transfiguration serves as something of a bridge between Christmas and Calvary, between Epiphany and Easter. Transfiguration contains echoes of the Lord's Baptism in the Father's voice from the cloud while at the same time pointing forward to his death and showing forth the glory of his resurrection. The Sundays of Lent draw us ever closer to Calvary with the Gradual based on Hebrews 12:2, "Oh, come, let us fix our eyes on Jesus, the author and perfector of our faith, who for the

---

201    *Lutheran Worship* (St. Louis: Concordia Publishing House, 1982), 6. For an exposition of *Gottesdienst* see *Lutheran Worship: History and Practice*, ed. Fred Precht (St. Louis: Concordia Publishing House, 1993), 44–45; Norman Nagel, "Whose Liturgy Is It?" *Logia* (Easter 1993): 4–8; Harold Senkbeil, *Dying to Live: The Power of the Forgiveness of Sins* (St. Louis: Concordia Publishing House, 1994), 115–36; John T. Pless, ed., *Real Life Worship Reader* (St. Louis: LCMS Commission on Worship, 1994).

joy set before him endured the cross, scorning its shame, and sat down at the right hand of the throne of God."

Historically, Holy Week is at the center of the Christian year, as the church year developed out of Easter, which, in turn, grew out of Sunday, the Lord's Day. It is often said that every Sunday is a little Easter. It is in fact more historically accurate to say that every Easter is a big Sunday. The traditional Epistle for the Feast of the Resurrection, 1 Corinthians 5:7–8, demonstrates the theological centrality of Good Friday–Easter to the whole of the church year: "Therefore purge out the old leaven, that you may be a new lump, since you truly are unleavened. For indeed Christ, our Passover, was sacrificed for us. Therefore let us keep the feast, not with old leaven nor with the leaven of malice and wickedness, but with the unleavened bread of sincerity and truth."

The remainder of the church year flows out of Good Friday–Easter, as can be seen from examining the Gospels appointed for the Sundays of Easter. In the Holy Gospel for the Second Sunday of Easter (John 20:19–31), the risen Lord comes to his disciples, speaking words of peace and showing them the tokens of his passion, his wounds. With his words and wounds, the Lord bestows on his disciples his Spirit and the apostolic office. The risen Lord is the source of life to his church just as the vine gives life to the branches in John 15:1–8, the Holy Gospel for Easter 3. Easter 4 is called Good Shepherd Sunday, since this Sunday's Gospel is John 10:11–16. The Gospels appointed for Easter 5 and 6 are from our Lord's farewell discourse on Maundy Thursday (John 16:4b–15 and 16:23b–33), and both connect the passion and resurrection with Ascension and Pentecost. The Holy Gospel for Pentecost (John 15:26–16:4) shows us that the gift of Pentecost is a reality because of the Lord's "going to the Father." The Sundays after Pentecost reflect the life of the crucified and risen Lord in the midst of his church as he enlivens and sustains his people by the gospel. The last Sundays of the church year point us to the consummation of Easter in the Lord's return to judge and the gift of the marriage supper of the Lamb in his kingdom.

The church year is a many-splendored reality. It has an integrity or a wholeness to it that centers in the work of the Liturgist of our salvation, Jesus Christ. This integrity provides a vehicle for an ongoing catechesis that is sometimes subtle but nonetheless real and potent. It is a shame, therefore, that we have allowed the church year to be replaced by the Synodical Year with its programmatic emphasis on the Christian's work rather than the work of the Trinity. This rejection of the church year signals a slippage away from grace to works. Our programs are deemed more beneficial to the life of the church than the story of salvation delivered systematically in the Christian year.

## SOME CONCLUDING OBSERVATIONS

(1) Each generation is "unwell in a new way," writes the poet John Berryman. In his book *The Contemplative Pastor*, Eugene Peterson argues that the present generation is "unwell" in that it is addicted to "episodes of adolescence." In other words, now the sins of the sons are being visited upon the fathers. Peterson writes, "There was a time when ideas and living styles were initiated in the adult world and filtered down to youth. Now the movement goes the other way: lifestyles are generated at the youth level and pushed upward. Dress fashions, hair styles, music, and morals that are adopted by youth are evangelically pushed on an adult world, which in turn seems eager to be converted."[202]

A major characteristic of the culture of adolescence is historical amnesia, the absence of a sense of the past. That which is old is thought to be obsolete. There is a temptation for the church to jettison its heritage in order to be relevant and in doing so capitulate to the idols of this present age. We need to take the warning of

---

202   Eugene Peterson, *The Contemplative Pastor* (Dallas: Word Publishing, 1989), 128–29.

Carl Braaten with utmost seriousness as he says, "The church that wants to be relevant has already sown the seeds of its own irrelevance."[203] If our children are to have faith, we must first of all be ourselves faithful to what we have been given. Simone Weil has said, "If you want to be relevant, you must always say things that are eternal."[204] Ours is not a cultural catechesis of pop psychology disguised as "relational Bible studies" and self-help books, of shallow songs that tell us more about the singer than they do about the triune God, of entertainment evangelisms that try to convince the pagans that we are just like them after all. Ours is a catechesis that is forever relevant because it is speaking eternal things, words of Him who is the Alpha and the Omega, in Scripture, Catechism, and liturgy. We are indeed to be countercultural in our ministry. Our catechesis will train both youth and adults to live as "resident aliens"[205] within a narcissistic religious culture.

> **If our children are to have faith, we must first of all be ourselves faithful to what we have been given.**

(2) In our work with youth we would do well to heed the remark of T. S. Eliot that "it is not enthusiasm but dogma that differentiates a Christian from a pagan."[206] In our desire "to make church fun" we have, in fact, trivialized the realities that we seek to pass on to our youth. Instead we are left with youth services that turn the Lord's Supper into a McDonald's Happy Meal and encourage our young people to have contempt for the allegedly boring and dull things that transpire in their home congregations at ten o'clock on Sunday morning.

(3) It is tempting to take shortcuts. But if we are to be about the task of feeding our Lord's sheep and caring for his lambs, then

---

203    Carl Braaten in a speech at St. Olaf College, Northfield, Minnesota, April 27, 1993.

204    Guinness, 6.

205    See Stanley Hauerwas and William Willimon, *Resident Aliens: Life in the Christian Colony* (Nashville: Abingdon Press, 1989).

206    Quoted by Robert Wilken, "No Other Gods," *First Things* (November 1993): 14.

we best use the equipment that he has bequeathed us: his word and sacraments. It is not given to us to entertain or excite, but faithfully to pass on the word that we have been given. And that word does have impressive power—power to create and preserve faith for the long haul, for see, the goal of catechesis is finally the resurrection of the body and life everlasting.

# Bibliography for Further Study of the Catechism

Arand, Charles. "Catechismal Services: A Bridge Between Evangelism and Assimilation." *Concordia Journal* (July 1997): 177–91.

———. "I Am God's Creature! Luther's Confession of the First Article of the Creed." In *From Wittenberg to the World: Essays in the Reformation and Its Legacy in Honor of Robert Kolb*. Edited by Charles Arand et al. Goettingen: Vandenhoeck & Ruprecht, 2018. 229–48.

———. "Luther on the God Behind the First Commandment." *Lutheran Quarterly* (Winter 1994): 397–424.

———. *That I May Be His Own: An Overview of Luther's Catechisms*. St. Louis: Concordia Publishing House, 2000.

Arand, Charles, Robert Kolb, and James Nestingen. *The Lutheran Confessions: History and Theology of the Book of Concord*. Minneapolis: Fortress Press, 2012.

Baker, Robert, editor. *Lutheran Spirituality: Life as God's Child*. St. Louis: Concordia Publishing House, 2010.

Bast, Robert James. *Honor Your Fathers: Catechisms and the Emergence of Patriarchal Ideology in Germany 1400–1600*. Leiden: Brill, 1997.

Bayer, Oswald. "The Doctrine of Justification and Ontology." *Neue Zeitschrift fuer Systematische Theologie und Religionsphilosphie* 43 (2001): 44–53.

———. "God's Omnipotence." *Lutheran Quarterly* (Spring 2009): 85–102.

———. "I Believe That God Has Created Me with All That Exists: An Example of Catechetical-Systematics." *Lutheran Quarterly* 8, no. 2 (Summer 1994): 129–61.

———. *Martin Luther's Theology: A Contemporary Interpretation.* Translated by Thomas H. Trapp. Grand Rapids: Eerdmans, 2003.

———. "The Plurality of the One God and the Plurality of the Gods." *Pro Ecclesia* (September 2006): 338–54.

Bender, Peter. *Lutheran Catechesis.* 2nd ed. Sussex: WI: Concordia Catechetical Academy, 2008.

Bode, Gerhard. "Instruction of the Christian Faith by Lutherans after Luther." In *Lutheran Ecclesiastical Culture 1550–1675.* Leiden: Brill, 2008. 159–204.

———. "Know How to Live and Die: Luther and the Teaching of the Christian Faith." *Concordia Journal* (Summer 2018): 15–33.

Bonhoeffer, Dietrich. *Psalms: The Prayer Book of the Bible.* Translated by James Burtness. Minneapolis: Augsburg Publishing House, 1970.

Bornkamm, Heinrich. *Luther in Mid-Career, 1521–1530.* Translated by E. Theodore Bachmann. Philadelphia: Fortress Press, 1983.

Bull, Bernard, editor. *The Pedagogy of Faith: Essays on Lutheran Education.* St. Louis: Concordia Publishing House, 2016.

Collver, Albert B. III, James Arne Nestingen, and John T. Pless, editors. *The Necessary Distinction: A Continuing Conversation on Law and Gospel.* St. Louis: Concordia Publishing House, 2017.

Fiala, David A. "Martin Luther's Small Catechism: A History of English Language Editions and Explanations Prepared by The Lutheran Church—Missouri Synod." *Concordia Historical Institute Quarterly* (Winter 2016): 29–49.

Forde, Gerhard O., and James Arne Nestingen. *Free to Be.* Minneapolis: Augsburg Publishing House, 1974.

Girgensohn, Herbert. *Teaching Luther's Catechisms*. 2 vols. Translated by John Doberstein. Philadelphia: Muhlenberg Press, 1959.

Haemig, Mary Jane. "Catechisms." In *Dictionary of Luther and the Lutheran Traditions*. Edited by Timothy Wengert. Grand Rapids: Baker Academic Press, 2017. 129–32.

———. "An Image of Luther for Today: The Catechetical Luther." *Word & World* (Spring 2016): 119–34.

———. "Praying amid Life's Perils: How Luther Used Biblical Examples to Teach Prayer." In *Encounters with Luther: New Directions for Critical Studies*. Edited by Kirsi I. Stjerna and Brooks Schramm. Louisville: Westminster/John Knox, 2016. 177–88.

———. "Preaching the Catechism: A Transformational Enterprise." *Dialog* 36 (1997): 133–45.

———. "Recovery Not Rejection: Luther's Appropriation of the Catechism." *Concordia Journal* (Winter/Spring 2017): 43–58.

Harran, Marilyn J. *Martin Luther: Learning for Life*. St. Louis: Concordia Publishing House, 1997.

Hinlicky, Paul R. *Luther for Evangelicals*. Grand Rapids: Baker Academic Press, 2018.

Iwand, Hans Joachim. "Die Predigt des Gesetzes." In *Glaubensgerechtigkeit: Gesammelte Ausfsaetze II*. Edited by Gerhard Sauter. Munich: Christian Kaiser, 1980.

Janz, Denis. *Three Reformation Catechisms: Catholic, Anabaptist, Lutheran*. New York: Edwin Mellen Press, 1982.

Juengel, Eberhard. *The Freedom of a Christian: Luther's Significance for Contemporary Theology*. Translated by Roy Harrisville. Minneapolis: Augsburg Publishing House, 1988.

Jurchen, Pete. *Timeless Truth: An Essential Guide for Teaching the Faith*. St. Louis: Concordia Publishing House, 2018.

———. "Why Luther's Small Catechism with Explanation Is a Tool Uniquely Suited for Parish Education." *Concordia Journal* (Summer 2018): 44–55.

Klug, Eugene F., translator and editor. *Sermons of Martin Luther: The House Postils.* 3 vols. Grand Rapids: Baker Book House, 1996.

Kolb, Robert. *Luther and the Stories of God: Biblical Narratives for Christian Living.* Grand Rapids: Baker Academic Press, 2012.

———. *Martin Luther: Confessor of the Faith.* Oxford: Oxford University Press, 2009.

———. *Teaching God's Children His Teaching: A Guide for the Study of Luther's Catechism* (Indian Edition). St. Louis: Luther Academy, 2004.

Kolb, Robert, and James Nestingen. *Sources and Contexts of the Book of Concord.* Minneapolis: Fortress Press, 2001.

Kolb, Robert, and Timothy Wengert, editors. *The Book of Concord.* Minneapolis: Fortress Press, 2000.

Korcok, Thomas. *Lutheran Education: From Wittenberg to the Future.* St. Louis: Concordia Publishing House, 2011.

Krause, Richard. "Remember the Saxon Visitation: Devotional Modeling for Christian Families" *Logia* (Reformation 2007): 21–28

Krodel, Gottfried. "Luther as Creative Writer: The Explanation of the Second Article of the Apostles' Creed in the Small Catechism." In *Ad Fontes Lutheri: Toward the Recovery of the Real Luther; Essays in Honor of Kenneth Hagen's Sixty-Fifth Birthday.* Edited by Timothy Maschke et al. Milwaukee: Marquette University Press, 2001. 130–64.

———. "Luther's Work on the Catechism in the Context of Late Medieval Catechetical Literature." *Concordia Journal* (October 1999): 364–404.

Leaver, Robin. "Luther's Catechism Hymns: The Ten Commandments." *Lutheran Quarterly* (Winter 1997): 411–22.

Leaver, Robin. *Luther's Liturgical Music: Principles and Implications.* Grand Rapids: Eerdmans, 2007.

Ludwig, Alan. "Preaching and Teaching the Creed: The Structure of the Small Catechism's Explanation as Guides." *Logia* (Reformation 1994): 11–24.

Mize, Gaven. *Beauty and Catechesis.* N.p. Grail Quest Books, 2017.

Nafzger, Samuel, editor. *Confessing the Gospel Today: A Lutheran Approach to Systematic Theology.* 2 vols. St. Louis: Concordia Publishing House, 2017.

Nelson, Derek R., and Paul R. Hinlicky, editors. *The Oxford Encyclopedia of Martin Luther.* 3 vols. Oxford: Oxford University Press, 2017.

Nestingen, James. "The Catechism's Simul." *Word & World* (Fall 1983): 364–72.

———. "Graven Images and Christian Freedom." *Lutheran Theological Journal* (May 2015): 27–33.

———. "The Lord's Prayer in Luther's Catechism." *Word & World* (Winter 2002): 36–48.

———. "Luther's Cultural Translation of the Catechism." *Lutheran Quarterly* (Winter 2001): 440–52.

———. *Martin Luther: A Life.* Minneapolis: Augsburg Fortress, 2003.

———. "Preaching the Catechism." *Word & World* (Winter 1990): 33–42.

Noll, Mark. *Confessions and Catechisms of the Reformation.* Vancouver: Regent College Press, 2004.

Nordling, John. "The Catechism: The Heart of the Reformation." *Logia* (Reformation 2007): 5–14.

Ozment, Steven. *When Fathers Ruled: Family Life in Reformation Europe.* Cambridge: Harvard University Press, 1983.

Paulson, Steven D. *Lutheran Theology.* London: T & T Clark, 2011.

Peters, Albrecht. *Commentary on Luther's Catechisms: Creed.* Translated by Thomas H. Trapp. St. Louis: Concordia Publishing House, 2011.

———. *Commentary on Luther's Catechisms: Baptism and Lord's Supper.* Translated by Thomas Trapp. St. Louis: Concordia Publishing House, 2012.

———. *Commentary on Luther's Catechisms: Confession and Christian Life.* Translated by Thomas H. Trapp. St. Louis: Concordia Publishing House, 2013.

———. *Commentary on Luther's Catechisms: Lord's Prayer.* Translated by Daniel Thies. St. Louis: Concordia Publishing House, 2011.

———. *Commentary on Luther's Catechisms: Ten Commandments.* Translated by Holger K. Sonntag. St. Louis: Concordia Publishing House, 2009.

Pless, John T. "Catechesis for Life in the Royal Priesthood." In *A Reader in Pastoral Theology.* Edited by John T. Pless. Fort Wayne: Concordia Theological Seminary Press, 2002. 63–70.

———. "Catechetical Discipleship." In *Handing Over the Goods: Essays in Honor Of James Arne Nestingen.* Edited by Steven D. Paulson and Scott L. Keith. Irvine: 1517 Publishing, 2018. 103–16.

———. "Catechism Foundations." In *Confirmation Basics.* Edited by Mark Sengele. St. Louis: Concordia Publishing House, 2009. 33–43.

———. "The Catechism: A Handbook for Times of Persecution." *The Lutheran Witness* (May 2017): 6–7.

———. "The Catechism as the Handbook for the Vocation of the Laity and Worship." *The Pieper Lectures: The Lutheran Doctrine of Vocation.* Edited by John A. Maxfield and Daniel Preus. St. Louis:

Concordia Historical Institute and The Luther Academy, 2008. 81–97.

———. "Catechisms, Luther's." In *Encyclopedia of Martin Luther and the Reformation*. Vol. 1: A–L. Edited by Mark A. Lamport. Lanham: Rowman & Littlefield, 2017. 109–110.

———. "Ceremonies for Seekers: Catechesis as a Fundamental Criterion for Worship in the Lutheran Confessions." In *Worship 2000*. Edited by John Maxfield and Jennifer Maxfield. St. Louis: The Luther Academy, 2010. 29–43.

———. *Didache*. Fort Wayne: Emmanuel Press, 2013.

———. "Fidelity to the Catechism in Prayer and Teaching." *Lutheran Forum* (Fall 2005): 8–15.

———. *Handling the Word of Truth: Law and Gospel in the Church Today*. Rev. ed. St. Louis: Concordia Publishing House, 2015.

———. *Martin Luther: Preacher of the Cross—A Study in Luther's Pastoral Theology*. St. Louis: Concordia Publishing House, 2013.

———. *Praying Luther's Small Catechism*. St. Louis: Concordia Publishing House, 2016.

———. "Preaching the Catechism—Part I." *Concordia Pulpit Resources* (May 30–August 29, 2010): 3–8.

———. "Preaching the Catechism—Part II." *Concordia Pulpit Resources* (September 5–November 21, 2010): 3–6.

———. "Reviewing Curriculum." In *Sunday School Basics*. Edited by Mark Sengele. St. Louis: Concordia Publishing House, 2005. 46–55.

———. "Sacraments in the Catechism: Treasures God Gives and Faith Receives." *Logia* (Holy Trinity 2017): 13–20.

———. *A Small Catechism on Human Life*. St. Louis: LCMS World Relief & Human Care, 2006.

Reu, J. Michel. *Catechetics*. Chicago: Wartburg Publishing House, 1927.

Russell, William R. *Praying for Reform: Luther, Prayer, and the Christian Life*. Minneapolis: Augsburg Fortress Press, 2005.

Sasse, Herman. *We Confess Jesus Christ*. Translated by Norman E. Nagel. St. Louis: Concordia Publishing House, 1984.

Schultz, Robert. "The Theological Significance of the Order of the Chief Parts in Luther's Catechism." In *Teaching the Faith: Luther's Catechisms in Perspective*. Edited by Carl Volz. River Forest: Lutheran Education Association, 1967.

Siggins, Ian. *Martin Luther's Doctrine of Christ*. New Haven: Yale University Press, 1970.

Steinmetz, David. "Luther and Formation in Faith." In *Educating People of Faith*. Edited by John van Engen. Grand Rapids: Eerdmans, 2004. 253–69.

Thompson, Virgil. "The Promise of Catechesis." *Lutheran Quarterly* (Autumn 1990): 259–70.

Truebenach, Kim A. "Luther's Two Kingdoms in the Third and Fourth Petitions." *Lutheran Quarterly* (Winter 2010): 469–73.

Trueman, Carl R. *Luther on the Christian Life: Cross and Freedom*. Wheaton: Crossways, 2015.

Vogel, Larry. "LCMS Catechism 6.0." *Concordia Journal* (Summer 2018): 34–43.

Wengert, Timothy J. "Fear and Love in the Ten Commandments." *Concordia Journal* (January 1995): 14–27.

———. *Martin Luther's Catechisms: Forming the Faith*. Minneapolis: Fortress Press, 2009.

———. "The Small Catechism, 1529." In *Pastoral Writings*. Vol. 4 of *The Annotated Luther*. Edited by Mary Jane Haemig. Minneapolis: Fortress Press, 2016. 201–52.

————. "Wittenberg's Earliest Catechism." *Lutheran Quarterly* (Autumn 1993): 247–60.

Wingren, Gustaf. *Luther on Vocation.* Translated by Carl C. Rasmussen. Philadelphia: Muhlenberg Press, 1957.

Zwanepol, Klaas. "The Structure and Dynamics of Luther's Catechism." *Acta Theologica* 31:2 (2011): 394–411.